LEARN TO READ
NEW TESTAMENT
GREEK
WORKBOOK

This workbook is dedicated to our Greek mentors & colleagues Dr. Wayne Brindle, Dr. James A. Freerksen, and Dr. James D. Stevens whose training equipped us to pursue this project and whose teaching caused our hearts to burn as they opened up to us the scriptures. We cannot thank you enough for investing your knowledge, time, and lives into us.

From Ben Gutierrez:

To my wife, Tammy:
Your commitment to your Lord,
family, and ministry
and your pattern of righteousness
is my eternal reminder of how fortunate
I am to have you in my life.

From Cara Murphy:

To my wonderful husband:
Even when great sacrifice was required,
you have always encouraged my passion
to pursue the original Word.
Psalm 78:72

LEARN TO READ
NEW TESTAMENT
GREEK
WORKBOOK

Supplemental Exercises for Greek Grammar Students

BEN GUTIERREZ AND CARA L. MURPHY

David A. Croteau, Managing Editor

ACADEMIC

NASHVILLE, TENNESSEE

Learn to Read New Testament Greek Workbook

© Copyright 2009 by Ben Gutierrez and Cara L. Murphy

Published by B&H Publishing Group
Nashville, Tennessee

ISBN: 978-0-8054-4792-7

Dewey Decimal Classification: 225.48
Subject Heading: GREEK LANGUAGE, BIBLICAL\BIBLE.N.T.GREEK

Printed in the United States of America

11 12 13 14 15 16 • 25 24 23 22 21
SB

CONTENTS

CHAPTER

PREFACE

An Encouragement to the Student

Choosing to study New Testament Greek is an exciting and life-changing journey! As you begin studying New Testament Greek, your understanding of the New Testament will grow in vividness and your passion to study His Word will grow exponentially! New Testament Greek will unfold the finer nuances of the Bible that will cause your mind to ponder its intricacies with a sense of awe and reverence. It is a worthy goal to become a wise exegete of God's holy Word. As you pursue your studies of New Testament Greek and work through this workbook, keep the following two encouragements in mind and allow them to energize and motivate you during this exciting journey!

Study New Testament Greek for the purpose of communing more intelligently and intimately with your Creator! Upon the outset, purpose in your heart that you will not allow self-glorifying reasons to be your motivation for studying New Testament Greek. Consider the ability to dissect and discern the finer nuances of God's holy Word through the careful utilization of New Testament Greek a privileged opportunity. Allow your training to translate into praise for the One who has given you the mind and the opportunity to study His precious Word. As you study, regularly ask yourself, "How can this grammatical, syntactical, or exegetical point translate not only on paper but into my daily walk as a servant of Jesus Christ?" Consciously look for ways that the study of New Testament Greek can positively affect the administration of your church, ministry, and home life. Allow what you learn in your study of New Testament Greek also to infuse your prayer life. Allow the truths of God that you extract in your study to cultivate an accuracy of doctrine and a sincerity of heart in your prayer life. With this perspective, you will grow in intimacy with your Creator and Savior!

Study New Testament Greek with this proven principle in mind: "No one is lazy and profound!" This mindset has motivated many students—including the authors of this workbook—to study diligently in order to receive rich blessings from God's Word. Studying New Testament Greek can be challenging at times. Undoubtedly, there will be seasons in your study that will cause you to contemplate giving up. You will have days when you will allow words of discouragement from others to resound more profoundly than they should. You will be tempted to rehearse the all-too-familiar words: "Well, I didn't study Greek, and I'm an OK preacher!" "All you have to do is use certain resources and you can know just as much as studying Greek!" "When you preach, you shouldn't use Greek anyway!" Admittedly, you do not need to know Greek in order to understand the essential truths of the Word of God, but Greek allows you to understand the finer, more vivid nuances present in His Word. It is this vividness that causes the hearers to be captivated with the teachings of the Word of God. It is this ability with Greek that will allow your listeners to *experience* the text and that will produce a contagious passion to study God's Word. Such ability takes time, energy, and endurance. Commit today to remain diligent in your study—even when the journey seems laborious. There is no doubt that God will honor your diligence in your study of New Testament Greek.

Helpful Tips for the Instructor

This workbook includes over 1,150 sentences (Greek to English/English to Greek), including about 225 participial sentences, and every form of every word in the sentences can be found within Greek writings in the New Testament era, from the Septuagint through the end of Revelation. Great care has been taken in forming each sentence. We attempted to capture as many grammatical constructions and considerations as a beginning Greek student may face in their study of New Testament Greek. In doing so, we have included more sentences than what may be possible to cover in class. We purposely provided an exorbitant amount of sentences so that the student could use this workbook for review *outside* of class as well as inside the classroom. There are enough sentences for the student to have a "fresh" review during various holiday breaks without having to rehearse previously translated sentences. Regarding sentences containing participles: most of the participial constructions are second attributive, substantival, or adverbial (temporal) constructions for easy and introductory learning of participles.

This workbook includes over 700 drilling exercises in order to reinforce the foundational principles of Greek verbs, nouns, adjectives, prepositions, definite articles, demonstrative pronouns, adverbs, conjunctions, and participles. The drilling exercises in this workbook include matching, true/false, fill-in-the-blank, short answer, transliterations, and exercises relevant to the study of New Testament Greek. The purpose of these drilling exercises is not to present every possible objective question that could possibly be asked of a beginning Greek student. The purpose of these drilling exercises is to reinforce the foundational principles explained in *Learn to Read New Testament Greek* (3rd edition; 2009) by David Alan Black. After these drilling exercises, most chapters then focus the attention of the student solely on sentence translation. The wording of these exercises parallels Black's book.

Each chapter includes the grammatical elements of previous chapters while emphasizing the specific grammatical element(s) identified in the specific chapter title. The sentences are unique to the authors but are categorized in concert with Black. The chapter titles of this workbook are taken from Black's textbook. The chapter numbers of this workbook parallel Black's textbook. Regardless of the Greek grammar textbook that a beginning Greek student consults, every beginning Greek student can benefit from the utilization of this workbook.

These sentences are "unpredictable." They were constructed in a thoughtful manner so that the student could not produce the final translation based on their familiarity with a certain Bible verse or even a predictable pattern of speech. Every sentence meets proper grammatical rules, but these sentences will cause Greek students to have to "fly by their instruments"! Just as a pilot has to trust his/her instruments upon losing visual clarity, the student will likewise be forced to follow rules of grammar when the sentences may not make too much "common sense." In addition, these sentences are simply for grammatical exercise. The sentences are not meant to make any particular theological statements or support any specific theological position.

This workbook does not contain an answer key to the sentences. This decision to omit the answer key from publication is profitable for the student for two major reasons. First, informal surveying of past Greek students has shown that at least a third of Greek students admitted to having a "serious" temptation to look at the "back of the book" in order to complete their translation homework (in one instance, over half of a class!!). Removing the answer key is an obvious deterrent to this specific temptation. We quickly recognized an additional benefit in removing the answer key from the workbook: in doing so, we are encouraging the student to confer with other students for help, discuss the problem at hand, grapple with it together, and produce a translation through teamwork. We see this as positive reinforcement that solidifies what the student learns in the classroom. In addition, we would encourage instructors to reserve the first few minutes in class to ask the students if they need clarity on a specific sentence. If you are an instructor and would like to have an answer key for your own reference, please contact the authors through Broadman and Holman at www.bhpublishinggroup.com/contact.asp to receive a complimentary answer key.

Consider taking your exam sentences directly from this workbook. If the student knows that you will possibly take your exam sentences directly from this workbook, he/she will be encouraged to translate the *entire* chapter. This should be encouraged! Even though it is possible for the student to have already translated the exam sentences, in doing so, they have translated over 100–300 additional sentences! If comprehension is the desired goal, taking exam sentences from this workbook could actually be a creative way to cultivate comprehension! If you are not comfortable with this, consider offering extra credit on an exam if a student translates a certain number of sentences from the workbook that were not assigned in class. For example, you could offer one percentage point of extra credit for every five sentences translated.

On the first day of class, encourage the students to read the "Encouragement to the Student" at the beginning of the preface. This will set a spiritual tone for why they should be studying New Testament Greek and will assist in reinforcing your own special encouragements that your present to them on the first day of class.

Constructive comments and reviews are always helpful and welcome. We welcome your comments regarding how to make this workbook a more effective tool for Greek students and instructors. If you have any constructive comments, we invite you to forward them to the authors through Broadman and Holman at www.bhpublishinggroup.com/contact.asp.

The Letters and Sounds of Greek

MATCHING

Match each term with the most appropriate option.

___ 1. phoneme

___ 2. morpheme

___ 3. diphthong

___ 4. rough breathing mark

___ 5. smooth breathing mark

___ 6. elision

___ 7. double consonant

___ 8. ν

___ 9. ρ

___ 10. acute accent

___ 11. θ, φ

___ 12. α, υ

___ 13. grave accent

___ 14. circumflex accent

___ 15. ς

A. two vowel phonemes joined to form a single sound

B. when a preposition's final vowel is replaced with an apostrophe before a word beginning with a vowel (e.g., διά = δι')

C. "rho"; makes "r" sound

D. Greek letters that are transliterated as two combined sounds (e.g. ψ is "ps")

E. examples: –ed, –ly, –ing

F. final sigma

G. the sounds represented by each corresponding letter of the Greek alphabet

H. '

I. "nu"; makes "n" sound

J. `

K. ^

L. ´

M. two aspirated consonants

N. ʽ

O. two letters that can form a diphthong

MULTIPLE CHOICE

Choose the best answer.

__ 1. Identify the Greek "theta."
   A. λ   B. φ   C. θ   D. ψ

__ 2. Identify the Greek "phi."

   A. χ   B. ρ   C. φ   D. γ

__ 3. Identify the Greek "eta."

   A. α   B. ε   C. η   D. ι

__ 4. The Greek alphabet contains _____ vowels.

   A. five   B. six   C. seven   D. eight

__ 5. Which of the following letters is considered a short vowel?

   A. η   B. ε   C. ω   D. ν

__ 6. Three of these vowels may either function as a long or short vowel. Which one does not belong?

   A. α   B. ι   C. υ   D. ο

__ 7. Which of the following is not a diphthong?

   A. ει   B. αυ   C. ια   D. ευ

__ 8. Which of the following is not an "improper" diphthong?

   A. ε   B. ᾳ   C. η   D. ῳ

__ 9. The "s" sound in Greek is considered a(n):

   A. aspirate   B. nasal   C. sibilant   D. bilabial

__10. The "h" sound in Greek is considered a(n):

   A. aspirate   B. nasal   C. sibilant   D. bilabial

TRUE/FALSE

Indicate whether the statement is true or false.

____ 1. Like English, Greek sentences always begin with a capital letter.

____ 2. A vowel with an iota subscript underneath is referred to as an improper diphthong.

____ 3. In an improper diphthong, the iota subscript is never pronounced.

____ 4. The breathing mark is always placed over the first vowel in a diphthong.

____ 5. Simply changing the accent over a Greek word could possibly change the meaning of that word.

SHORT ANSWER

Provide a brief answer for each question.

1. Write the corresponding Greek *punctuation* mark:

   comma   _____

   period   _____

   colon   _____

   question mark _____

2. Write the corresponding Greek *accent* mark:

   acute   _____

   grave   _____

   circumflex   _____

3. List all seven proper (or "common") diphthongs.

   _____

4. List all three improper diphthongs.

   _____

5. Write out the Greek alphabet twenty times (including both forms of sigma).

Transliteration Key

α = a

β = b

γ = g

γ = n (if it precedes γ, κ, ξ, χ)

δ = d

ε = e

ζ = z

η = ē

θ = th

ι = i

κ = k

λ = l

μ = m

ν = n

ξ = x

ο = o

π = p

ρ = r

σ/ς = s

τ = t

υ = u (if used in a diphthong)

υ = y (if not in a diphthong)

φ = ph

χ = ch

ψ = ps

ω = ō

Additional Rules of Transliteration

- Rough breathing mark = h

    Precedes a vowel (example: ἑ = he; αἱ = hai)

    Follows an r (example: ῥ = rh)

- Accents/smooth breathing marks/iota subscripts = [not shown in transliteration]

Transliterate the following English renderings into Greek.

1. charis ("grace")

2. pisteuō ("I believe")

3. sesōsmenoi ("have been saved")

4. apostoloi ("apostles")

5. mathētēs ("disciple")

6. sōzetai ("he is being saved")

7. Paulos ("Paul")

8. dikaiosunē ("righteousness")

9. proseuchomai ("I pray")

10. logos ("word")

11. huios ("son")

12. ergon ("work")

13. hodos ("road")

14. hēmera ("day")

15. exousia ("authority")

16. hōra ("hour")

17. agapē ("love")

18. hypokritēs ("hypocrite")

19. ho logos theou estin agathos ("The word of God is good.")

_____

20. elyou hypo tou kyriou ("You [sg.] were being loosed by the Lord.")

_____

Transliterate the following Greek words into English.

1. Χριστός (Christ)

2. θεός (God)

3. φωνῆ (to a voice/sound)

4. ἀκούσουσιν (they will hear)

5. ἀγαπάω (I love)

6. φιλέω (I love)

7. κύριος (lord, master)

8. ἄγγελοι (angels, messengers)

9. ψυχή (soul, spirit)

10. ἡτοίμασεν (he/she/it prepared)

11. ἀπόστολος (apostle)

12. ταῦτα (these [things])

13. σεσωσμένοι (have been saved)

14. λυθήσεται (he/she/it will be loosed)

15. αἷμα (blood)

16. ῥῆμα (word, saying)

17. φιλῶ σε. (I love you.)

18. εἶ σεσωσμένος; (Are you saved?)

_____

19. Ἰησοῦς ἀγαπᾷ ὑμᾶς. (Jesus loves you [pl.].)

_____

20. εἰμι ἡ ὁδὸς, ἡ ἀλήθεια, καὶ ἡ ζωή. (I am the way, the truth, and the life.)

_____

2

THE GREEK VERB SYSTEM: A BIRD'S EYE VIEW

MATCHING:

Match each term with the most appropriate option.

____ 1. imperfective aspect

    A. related patterns of verbs

____ 2. aoristic aspect

    B. a verb that functions as the basic verbal element of a clause

____ 3. inflection

    C. the manner in which the speaker relates the verbal idea to reality

____ 4. primary tenses

    D. verbal stem

____ 5. lexical morpheme

    E. when the speaker affirms the factuality of the statement; the mood of reality

____ 6. finite verb

    F. "I love"

____ 7. mood

    G. when a verb expresses a command

____ 8. indicative mood

    H. "I am loving"

____ 9. imperative mood

    I. when a verb expresses contingency

____ 10. subjunctive mood

    J. when a verb expresses a verbal idea without limiting it by specifying person and number

____ 11. infinitive mood

    K. present, future, perfect, and future perfect

____ 12. voice

    L. the way in which the speaker chooses to relate the grammatical subject of a verb to the action of that verb

MULTIPLE CHOICE

Choose the best answer.

____ 1. Which type of word makes a statement about a subject or transfers an action from the subject to an object?
A. noun   B. adjective   C. verb   D. preposition

____ 2. Which of the following English phrases represents "third person"?

A. "I have"   B. "he has"   C. "we have"   D. "you have"

____ 3. Which of the following English phrases represents "perfective" aspect?

A. "I was loving"   B. "I loved"   C. "I will love"   D. "I will have loved"

____ 4. Which of the following English phrases represents "second person"?

A. "I have"   B. "he has"   C. "we have"   D. "you have"

____ 5. Which of the following voices makes the subject appear to be acting in its own interest?

A. middle   B. passive   C. active   D. none

____ 6. Which of the following is the lexical morpheme of the Greek word ἔχομεν?

A. -μεν   B. -ο-   C. ἔχ-   D. none of the above

____ 7. Which of the following is the person-number suffix of the Greek word ἔχομεν?

A. -μεν   B. -ο-   C. ἔχ-   D. none of the above

____ 8. Which of the following voices makes the subject to be the one acted upon ((i.e., makes the subject to be the recipient of the action)?

A. middle   B. passive   C. active   D. none

____ 9. Which of the following is considered a composite tense (see §15)?

A. "I ate"   B. "He eats"   C. "We eat"   D. "You have eaten"

___10. Which of the following terms refers to moods that are not indicative?

A. actual   B. unmarked   C. factual   D. potential

TRUE/FALSE

Indicate whether the statement is true or false.

____ 1. A verb stem contains the lexical or dictionary meaning of the word.

____ 2. The active voice highlights the grammatical subject of a sentence, and the middle and passive voices highlight the action of the verb.

____ 3. The term *aspect* refers to the view of the action that the speaker chooses to present to the hearer.

____ 4. The present, future, pluperfect, and future perfect are sometimes called secondary (or historical) tenses.

____ 5. Tense in Greek is determined by the writer's portrayal of the action with regard to aspect and (in the indicative mood) to time.

____ 6. The imperfect, aorist, and pluperfect are sometimes called primary (or principal) tenses.

____ 7. A clause is a group of words forming a sense unit and containing at least one finite verb.

____ 8. The term *mood* comes from the Latin *modus*, meaning "measure" or "manner."

____ 9. The English sentence "Mark has dressed himself" expresses the function of the passive voice.

____ 10. When present or past tense English verbs are formed together with some part of "will," "have," or "be," the result is an auxiliary verb.

SHORT ANSWER

Provide a brief answer for each question.

1. Read the following sentences and identify what verbal aspect (aoristic, perfective, imperfective) is being expressed by the italicized verbs:

   a.   Mary *has cooked* dinner for the entire family.

        Answer: _____

   b.   Anthony *is making* a lot of money at his new job.

        Answer: _____

   c.   John *wrote* a poem for his English class.

        Answer: _____

   d.   Carol *sits* on her rocking chair.

        Answer: _____

2. In your own words, describe the significance of tense (aspect) for reading Greek.

3. After reading this lesson, would you consider Greek to be a more or less specific (inflected) language than English?

4. Explain the importance of *mood* in Greek. Provide more than just the definition.

3

PRESENT AND FUTURE ACTIVE INDICATIVE

MATCHING

Match each term with the most appropriate option.

_____ 1. amalgamation

_____ 2. simple present use of λύω

_____ 3. present active principal part

_____ 4. conjugation

_____ 5. future time morpheme

_____ 6. "I am"

_____ 7. primary active suffixes

_____ 8. internal subject

_____ 9. copulative verb

_____ 10. connecting vowel

_____ 11. future active principal part

A.

SING	PLUR
-ω	-μεν
-εις	-τε
-ει	-ουσι(ν)

B. an additive letter that functions as a phonological cushion between the verb stem and suffix

C. the translation for the most frequently occurring verb in the -μι conjugation

D. the first person singular form λύσω

E. a phonological change that occurs when the future time morpheme σ is attached to the stem of the verb

F. the subject of the verb included within the verbal structure

G. a verb that links subject and predicate

H. the term that refers to "related patterns of verbs"

I. the first person singular form λύω

J. σ

K. "I loose"

MULTIPLE CHOICE

Choose the best answer.

____ 1. In the indicative mood, the primary tenses deal with

A. present time   B. past time   C. future time   D. both A and C

____ 2. The future time morpheme σ is equivalent to the English word

A. "been"   B. "was"   C. "will"   D. "have"

____ 3. When one of the consonants π, β, φ amalgamate with the future time morpheme (σ), they combine to form which consonant?

A. ζ   B. ξ   C. ψ   D. σ

____ 4. When one of the consonants κ, γ, χ amalgamate with the future time morpheme (σ), they combine to form which consonant?

A. ζ   B. ξ   C. ψ   D. σ

____ 5. When one of the consonants τ, δ, θ amalgamate with the future time morpheme (σ), they combine to form which consonant?

A. ξ   B. ψ   C. σ   D. τ, δ, θ drop out

____ 6. The phoneme that is occasionally added to the third person form of a verb is called

A. movable τ   B. movable ν   C. movable ρ   D. movable π

____ 7. Slightly differing forms of a morpheme (e.g., -ουσι and -ουσιν) are called

A. phonemes   B. allomorphs   C. transformers   D. suffix amalgamations

____ 8. It is possible for a present active indicative verb to denote what kind of action?

A. aoristic   B. imperfective   C. both   D. neither

____ 9. It is possible for a future active indicative verb to denote what kind of action?

A. aoristic   B. imperfective   C. both   D. neither

____10. What "voice" is the Greek verb εἰμί ("I am") technically spoken in?

A. active voice   B. passive voice   C. both   D. no voice

TRUE/FALSE

Indicate whether the statement is true or false.

____ 1. The connecting vowel is sometimes referred to as a neutral morpheme.

____ 2. When an external subject for a verb is given, the internal subject is translated first.

____ 3. Person-number (pronoun) suffixes indicate masculine, feminine, and neuter gender.

____ 4. The copulative verb εἰμί expresses a state of being rather than an action.

____ 5. The negative οὐ is usually used with the indicative mood.

____ 6. The source of a verb is always its future form.

____ 7. Negatives come *after* the word to which they refer.

____ 8. The allomorph -ουσιν is more emphatic than the allomorph -ουσι.

____ 9. When added to a word, a neutral morpheme does not affect the meaning of a verb.

____ 10. In the sentence, "Jesus looses," the word "Jesus" is considered an external subject.

SHORT ANSWER

Provide a brief answer for each question.

1. There are six elements identified when parsing a verb. Name all six.

2. The term *aspect* refers to the view of the action that the speaker chooses to present to the hearer. Name the three categories of aspect.

3. Following grammatical rules, draw a line from the negative adverb to its corresponding verb.

οὐ	ἑτοιμάζω
οὐκ	λύω
οὐχ	ἀκούω

DRILLS and EXERCISES

CONJUGATIONS

Conjugate the present active indicative forms for "I send."

_____   _____

_____   _____

_____   _____

Conjugate the present active indicative forms for "I prepare."

_____   _____

_____   _____

_____   _____

Conjugate the future active indicative forms for "I have."

_____   _____

_____   _____

_____   _____

Conjugate the future active indicative forms for "I heal."

_____   _____

_____   _____

_____   _____

Conjugate the present indicative forms for "I am."

_____   _____

_____   _____

_____   _____

TRANSLATIONS

Provide both an aoristic and imperfective translation for the following Greek words:

Greek Word	Aoristic Translation	Imperfective Translation
λύει	_____	_____
πείθομεν	_____	_____
ἕξω	_____	_____
ἄγετε	_____	_____
πέμψει	_____	_____
σώσω	_____	_____
δοξάζει	_____	_____
γράψεις	_____	_____
ἑτοιμάσω	_____	_____
πιστεύουσιν	_____	_____
θεραπεύσει	_____	_____
ἀκούετε	_____	_____
βαπτίσει	_____	_____
ἕξομεν	_____	_____

ANALYZE

The following Greek verbs have been divided into various components that make up the Greek verb. Label each component using its grammatical term/label. One example is done for you, namely, "λύσομεν."

Future Time Morpheme   *Connecting Vowel/Neutral Morpheme*

λύ|σ|ό|μεν

Lexical morpheme   *Primary Active Suffix*

ἀκούσετε

ἔχω

ἐστίν

βλέπει

πείθομεν

κηρύσσετε

σώζει

πιστεύσουσιν

PARSING

Parse the following Greek words:

	πείθεις	εἰμί	βαπτίσει	κηρύσσουσιν	κηρύξεις	ἀκούομεν
1. Tense	_____	_____	_____	_____	_____	_____
2. Voice	_____	_____	_____	_____	_____	_____
3. Mood	_____	_____	_____	_____	_____	_____
4. Person	_____	_____	_____	_____	_____	_____
5. Number	_____	_____	_____	_____	_____	_____
6. Source	_____	_____	_____	_____	_____	_____

	ἄξεις	ἕξεις	γράψω	εἶ	ἐστί	βλέπουσιν
1. Tense	_____	_____	_____	_____	_____	_____
2. Voice	_____	_____	_____	_____	_____	_____
3. Mood	_____	_____	_____	_____	_____	_____
4. Person	_____	_____	_____	_____	_____	_____
5. Number	_____	_____	_____	_____	_____	_____
6. Source	_____	_____	_____	_____	_____	_____

	εἰσίν	θεραπεύσω	we loose	we are loosing	she will save	I am
1. Tense	_____	_____	_____	_____	_____	_____
2. Voice	_____	_____	_____	_____	_____	_____
3. Mood	_____	_____	_____	_____	_____	_____
4. Person	_____	_____	_____	_____	_____	_____
5. Number	_____	_____	_____	_____	_____	_____
6. Source	_____	_____	_____	_____	_____	_____

PUTTING IT ALL TOGETHER!!

Using the Greek word provided below, practice doing all of the following exercises.

λύσεις

ANALYZE

*Divide this Greek word into its various components and label
each component with its grammatical term/label.*

PARSE

*Provide the generic parsing elements in left-hand column (in order) and corresponding
parsing elements for the Greek word provided in the right-hand column.*

1. _____ : _____

2. _____ : _____

3. _____ : _____

4. _____ : _____

5. _____ : _____

6. _____ : _____

TRANSLATE

Aoristically   _____

Imperfectively   _____

Putting It All Together!!

Using the Greek word provided below, practice doing all of the following exercises.

ἀκούσουσιν

Analyze

Divide this Greek word into its various components and label each component with its grammatical term/label.

Parse

Provide the generic parsing elements in left-hand column (in order) and corresponding parsing elements for the Greek word provided in the right-hand column.

1. _____ : _____

2. _____ : _____

3. _____ : _____

4. _____ : _____

5. _____ : _____

6. _____ : _____

Translate

Aoristically   _____

Imperfectively   _____

PUTTING IT ALL TOGETHER!!

Using the Greek word provided below, practice doing all of the following exercises.

κηρύσσει

ANALYZE

*Divide this Greek word into its various components
and label each component with its grammatical term/label.*

PARSE

*Provide the generic parsing elements in left-hand column (in order) and corresponding parsing
elements for the Greek word provided in the right-hand column.*

1. _____ : _____

2. _____ : _____

3. _____ : _____

4. _____ : _____

5. _____ : _____

6. _____ : _____

TRANSLATE

Aoristically   _____

Imperfectively   _____

PUTTING IT ALL TOGETHER!!

Using the Greek word provided below, practice doing all of the following exercises.

σῴζετε

ANALYZE

*Divide this Greek word into its various components and label
each component with its grammatical term/label.*

PARSE

*Provide the generic parsing elements in left-hand column (in order) and corresponding
parsing elements for the Greek word provided in the right-hand column.*

1. _____ : _____

2. _____ : _____

3. _____ : _____

4. _____ : _____

5. _____ : _____

6. _____ : _____

TRANSLATE

Aoristically   _____

Imperfectively   _____

PUTTING IT ALL TOGETHER!!

Using the Greek word provided below, practice doing all of the following exercises.

πείθεις

ANALYZE

*Divide this Greek word into its various components and label
each component with its grammatical term/label.*

PARSE

*Provide the generic parsing elements in left-hand column (in order) and corresponding
parsing elements for the Greek word provided in the right-hand column.*

1. _____ : _____

2. _____ : _____

3. _____ : _____

4. _____ : _____

5. _____ : _____

6. _____ : _____

TRANSLATE

Aoristically   _____

Imperfectively   _____

PUTTING IT ALL TOGETHER!!

Using the Greek word provided below, practice doing all of the following exercises.

ἑτοιμάζουσιν

ANALYZE

Divide this Greek word into its various components and label each component with its grammatical term/label.

PARSE

Provide the generic parsing elements in left-hand column (in order) and corresponding parsing elements for the Greek word provided in the right-hand column.

1. _____ : _____

2. _____ : _____

3. _____ : _____

4. _____ : _____

5. _____ : _____

6. _____ : _____

TRANSLATE

Aoristically _____

Imperfectively _____

GREEK to ENGLISH

Provide the English translation for each Greek sentence.

1. λύουσιν. λύσετε. οὐ λύει. οὐ λύετε.

   _____

2. ἀκούετε. ἀκούεις. ἀκούσουσιν. ἀκούσουσιν;

   _____

3. διδάσκω. διδάξει. δοξάζω. δοξάσει.

   _____

4. οὐκ ἄγει. οὐκ ἐστίν. οὐχ ἕξομεν. οὐχ ἕξομεν;

   _____

5. διδάσκεις. οὐ δοξάσει; δοξάσει. σώσω.

   _____

6. ἔχετε; θεραπεύσει. οὐχ ἑτοιμάσουσιν. λύσουσιν.

   _____

7. εἰσίν. οὐκ εἰμί. οὐ πείσομεν. οὐ πιστεύει;

   _____

8. οὐ βαπτίζει. σώσει. κηρύσσει. οὐ κηρύξεις.

   _____

9. κηρύξω; οὐ γράψεις. οὐχ ἑτοιμάσουσιν; λύει.

   _____

10. οὐχ ἕξεις. οὐκ ἄξεις. οὐκ ἄξεις; οὐχ ἕξεις;

    _____

11. οὐκ ἀκούσει. βαπτίζεις. πέμψουσιν; οὐ βλέψετε.

    _____

12. ἄξουσιν. διδάξω. οὐ λύσουσιν. λύετε;

    _____

13. οὐ λύει. οὐκ ἄγουσιν. οὐχ ἕξομεν. πείθεις.

    _____

14. γράψεις. οὐ πείσω. σώσουσιν. βαπτίσει.

    _____

15. εἰμί. εἶ. εἰμί; εἶ;

    _____

16. οὐχ ἑτοιμάζω. οὐχ ἕξω; κηρύσσουσιν. οὐ πιστεύω.

_____

17. διδάξουσιν; δοξάσουσιν. διδάξεις. δοξάζω.

_____

18. οὐ πείσω; οὐ πιστεύσεις; οὐ πέμπει. οὐ θεραπεύετε.

_____

19. βλέπουσιν; ἀκούσουσιν. οὐχ ἕξει. οὐ σώζεις.

_____

20. οὐ δοξάζει. κηρύξεις. οὐ κηρύξεις; οὐκ εἰσίν.

_____

21. σώσετε; πέμπει. πείσομεν. οὐ γράψω.

_____

22. οὐ θεραπεύσω. ἐστίν. οὐκ ἐστέ. οὐκ εἶ.

_____

23. ἑτοιμάσουσιν; κηρύσσει. οὐ δοξάσουσιν. σώσουσιν.

_____

24. πείθομεν. οὐχ ἕξω. οὐκ ἄξει. βαπτίσει;

_____

25. οὐ βλέψετε. βλέπεις.

_____

26. ἄγετε. ἄξει.

_____

27. γράφομεν. οὐ γράψει;

_____

28. δοξάζετε. δοξάσεις;

_____

29. ἑτοιμάζουσιν. ἑτοιμάσεις.

_____

30. ἔχετε. ἔχουσιν.

_____

ENGLISH to GREEK

Provide the Greek translation for each English sentence.

1. You (pl.) heal. I do not loose.

   _____

2. I will trust in. You (pl.) will write.

   _____

3. They do not send. You (sg.) are.

   _____

4. I loose. I am loosing.

   _____

5. You (sg.) do not trust in. You (pl.) will not believe.

   _____

6. I am healing. Will we not baptize?

   _____

7. I will preach. They will not heal. Will you (pl.) not preach?

   _____

8. He does not prepare. You (sg.) have. Does it not save?

   _____

9. Do we loose? Are we loosing? He has. He is having.

   _____

10. We will not lead. Will we not lead? He teaches.

    _____

11. I am saving. He trusts in. It does not believe.

    _____

12. Will we heal? Will I prepare? I do not prepare.

    _____

13. You (sg.) will teach. You (pl.) do not glorify. They will write.

    _____

14. We will not have. You (sg.) are not. Are you (pl.) not?

    _____

15. Will I loose? Am I loosing? Will you (pl.) heal?

    _____

16. You (pl.) will send. You (sg.) baptize. I do not loose.

_____

17. They will believe. We will glorify. They will not hear.

_____

18. He glorifies. She writes. It hears.

_____

19. It will send. You (pl.) will have. She will hear.

_____

20. It will not send. You (pl.) will not have. She will not hear.

_____

Nouns of the Second Declension

MATCHING

Match each term with the most appropriate option.

____ 1. declension	A. represents the subject
____ 2. case form	B. connects the noun with the case-number suffix
____ 3. nominative	C. the inflection of a noun
____ 4. genitive	D. a noun *with* a definite article
____ 5. dative	E. indicates whether a part of speech is masculine, feminine, or neuter
____ 6. accusative	F. a noun *without* a definite article
____ 7. vocative	G. represents the person or thing addressed
____ 8. case-number suffix	H. a conjunction that cannot stand first in its clause or sentence
____ 9. stem vowel	I. decides the function of a noun (i.e., subject, object, etc.)
____ 10. gender	J. represents the indirect object
____ 11. arthrous	K. often represents the possessor
____ 12. anarthrous	L. represents the direct object
____ 13. coordinate conjunction	M. a conjunction that presents dependent clauses
____ 14. subordinate conjunction	N. a conjunction that unites corresponding words or clauses
____ 15. postpositive	O. endings attached to a noun indicating its position and quantity

MULTIPLE CHOICE

Choose the best answer.

___ 1. An example of the locative dative is

    A. "in a man"   B. "for a man"   C. "by a man"   D. "from a man"

___ 2. An example of the instrumental dative is

    A. "in a man"   B. "for a man"   C. "by a man"   D. "from a man"

___ 3. An example of the dative of personal advantage is

    A. "in a man"   B. "for a man"   C. "by a man"   D. "from a man"

___ 4. An example of the ablatival genitive is

    A. "in a man"   B. "for a man"   C. "by a man"   D. "from a man"

___ 5. εἰμί requires a noun complement in the ___ case.

    A. nominative   B. genitive   C. dative   D. accusative

___ 6. The Greek indefinite article is ___.

    A. η   B. ο   C. ι   D. nonexistent

___ 7. ὄχλος, meaning "crowd," indicates ___ gender.

    A. masculine   B. feminine   C. neuter   D. both A and B

___ 8. ἔργον, meaning "work," indicates ___ gender.

    A. masculine   B. feminine   C. neuter   D. both A and B

___ 9. ὁδός, meaning "road, way," indicates ___ gender.

    A. masculine   B. feminine   C. neuter   D. both A and B

TRUE/FALSE

Choose whether the statement is true or false.

___ 1. Neuter plural nouns regularly take singular verbs.

___ 2. A noun can belong in more than one declension.

___ 3. In Greek, definite and indefinite articles are the same word, and only context can determine how the word is used in the sentence.

___ 4. A postpositive word is regularly seen as the second word in a Greek clause but should be translated first in an English sentence.

___ 5. In Greek, the word order of the sentence determines the grammatical role (subject, direct object, etc.) of a particular noun in the sentence.

SHORT ANSWER

Provide a brief answer for each question.

The six parsing elements for nouns that will be used throughout this workbook are as follows:

    1. Part of Speech (whether the Greek word is a noun, adjective, etc.)
    2. Declension (1st, 2nd, or 3rd)
    3. Gender (masculine, feminine, or neuter)
    4. Number (singular or plural)
    5. Case (nominative, genitive, dative, accusative)
    6. Source (the lexical form of the Greek word)

Your professor may decide to change some of these elements, but these six will be useful in order to complete the exercises on the following pages.

    1. Parse ἄνθρωπος.

    2. Parse ὁδός.

3. List all of the case-number suffixes for both the *masculine* and *neuter* nouns of the second declension.

Masculine   **Neuter**

Masculine	Neuter
_____	_____
_____	_____
_____	_____
_____	_____
_____	_____
_____	_____
_____	_____

4.   Decline υἱός below   Decline τέκνον below

_____	_____
_____	_____
_____	_____
_____	_____
_____	_____
_____	_____

5. Identify which word(s) within the following English sentences would be in the nominative, genitive, dative, and accusative cases.

NOTE: Place an "X" on the line if that particular case is not represented in the sentence.

"Joe pushed the man of God."

       Nominative _____

       Genitive   _____

       Dative   _____

       Accusative _____

"Jesus preached the truth to the people of the world."

       Nominative _____

       Genitive   _____

       Dative   _____

       Accusative _____

"The Word of God will convict men and women."

       Nominative _____

       Genitive   _____

       Dative   _____

       Accusative _____

"I answer God."

       Nominative _____

       Genitive   _____

       Dative   _____

       Accusative _____

Greek to English

Provide the English translation for each Greek sentence.

1. λύετε δούλους, ἀλλὰ λύσω τέκνα.

   _____

   _____

2. ἀδελφός πείσει θεόν, καὶ Χριστὸς σώσει ἀδελφόν.

   _____

   _____

3. βλέπει τέκνον ἀδελφόν, ἀλλ' ἀδελφὸς πέμψει τέκνον ἱερῷ.

   _____

   _____

4. ἔχω νόμον, ἀλλ' ἔχεις λόγους θεοῦ.

   _____

   _____

5. πέμψουσιν υἱοὶ δῶρα διακόνοις;

   _____

   _____

6. ἄγγελοί εἰσιν διάκονοι θεοῦ, καὶ θεὸς γινώσκει διακόνους.

   _____

   _____

7. βαπτίσει ἄνθρωπος θεοῦ ὄχλον ἁμαρτωλῶν, ἀλλὰ τέκνα οὐ βλέπει ἁμαρτωλούς.

   _____

   _____

8. Ἰησοῦς ἐστι καὶ κύριος καὶ Χριστὸς καὶ βλέψετε ἔργα θεοῦ.

   _____

   _____

9. ἄξει ἀπόστολος ἁμαρτωλοὺς Χριστῷ, οὐ δὲ διδάξει τέκνα.

   _____

   _____

10. δοξάσει τέκνα νόμον ἁμαρτωλῶν, καὶ οὐκ ἄξεις τέκνα ἱερῷ θεοῦ.

    _____

    _____

11. οὐκ ἀκούσουσιν ἀδελφόν, θεραπεύσω δὲ δοῦλον.

    _____

    _____

12. δῶρον θεοῦ ἐστι Χριστὸς Ἰησοῦς.

    _____

    _____

13. οὐκ ἔχει κόσμος εὐαγγέλιον καὶ ἕξουσιν ἁμαρτωλοὶ ὁδὸν θανάτου.

    _____

    _____

14. οὐ γινώσκουσιν θεοὶ λίθου ὁδὸν θεῷ, ἀλλ᾽ κηρύξω Χριστὸν ἁμαρτωλοῖς.

    _____

    _____

15. φέρω δῶρα οἴκῳ δούλων, ἀλλ᾽ οὐ βλέψετε θεόν.

    _____

    _____

16. οὐ λαμβάνει ὄχλος λόγους Ἰησοῦ, καὶ οὐ κηρύσσει λόγους Ἰησοῦ τέκνοις.

    _____

    _____

17. εἰμὶ ἁμαρτωλός, θεὸς δὲ σῴζει ἁμαρτωλούς.

    _____

    _____

18. ἔργα νόμου οὐ σώσουσιν ἀνθρώπους, καὶ ἔργα ἀνθρώπων οὐ θεραπεύσουσιν ἀνθρώπους.

    _____

    _____

19. ἄνθρωποι λαμβάνουσιν δῶρα θεοῦ, ἀλλ᾽ ἔξω ἀγροὺς λίθων.

20. γινώσκεις ᾽Ιησοῦν Χριστόν; ᾽Ιησοῦς Χριστὸς γινώσκει τέκνον θεοῦ;

21. ἄνθρωπος λέγει λόγους θεοῦ καὶ βαπτίσει ἀδελφούς.

22. λαμβάνετε εὐαγγέλιον, ἀλλ᾽ ἔργον θεοῦ φέρει δῶρα ἀνθρώποις.

23. κηρύσσει οἶκος θεοῦ λόγους Χριστοῦ, καὶ τέκνα θεοῦ πιστεύσει ᾽Ιησοῦν.

24. διδάξει τέκνα θεοῦ ἁμαρτωλούς, καὶ βλέψετε ἔργα θεοῦ.

25. φέρουσιν λόγοι ἁμαρτωλῶν θάνατον, φέρω δὲ δῶρα θεοῦ ἀνθρώποις.

26. λέγει ἄνθρωπος εὐαγγέλιον τέκνῳ, ἀλλ᾽ οὐκ ἀκούσουσιν ὄχλοι τέκνον.

27. ᾽Ιησοῦς οὐ πέμψει καὶ διακόνους καὶ ὄχλους, θεραπεύσει δὲ ἀγγέλους θεοῦ.

28. φέρει ἔργα ἁμαρτωλῶν θάνατον, Χριστὸς δὲ γινώσκει δούλους θεοῦ.

   _____

   _____

29. εἶ ἄνθρωπος θεοῦ, ἀλλὰ πέμψει ἄνθρωπος θεοῦ δῶρα θεοῦ καὶ ἀγγέλοις καὶ ἀποστόλοις.

   _____

   _____

30. λέγει ἄνθρωπος λόγους εὐαγγελίου υἱῷ ἀνθρώπων, οὐ δὲ εἰμὶ δοῦλος θεοῦ.

   _____

   _____

ENGLISH to GREEK

Provide the Greek translation for each English sentence.

1. I prepare ministers of a gospel.

   _____

   _____

2. Will slaves see both gifts and a law?

   _____

   _____

3. A son knows words of God.

   _____

   _____

4. I glorify God, but you (sg.) will lead a sinner to death.

   _____

   _____

5. He has houses of stone, but I have a temple.

   _____

   _____

6. Will we baptize both sinners and brothers?

_____

_____

7. A work of Christ is a gift of God.

_____

_____

8. Angels of God bring good news to men.

_____

_____

9. Jesus Christ is not a God of death.

_____

_____

10. Apostles will teach a law of Jesus.

_____

_____

11. Both children and men know a world of death.

_____

_____

12. Do you (pl.) bring gifts to men?

_____

_____

13. I take a word to both houses and a temple.

_____

_____

14. A temple of men will baptize lords of stone.

_____

_____

15. Christ is Lord, but man is a sinner.

_____

_____

16. A house and a field are gifts of God.

_____

_____

17. Will not a gospel of Jesus save sinners?

_____

_____

18. You (pl.) know a law of God, but I do not know Christ.

_____

_____

19. We are gifts of Jesus, but you (sg.) do not know God.

_____

_____

20. Crowds will not have a law of death.

_____

_____

1st and 2nd Declension Noun Endings

Description	**Declension**	2nd	2nd	1st	1st	1st	1st	1st
	Gender	Masc	Neut	Fem	Fem	Fem	Masc	Masc
	Stem Ending	—	—	ε, ι, ρ	Sibilant	Other	Other	ε, ι, ρ
	Key Word	ἄνθρωπος	δῶρον	ἡμέρα	δόξα	φωνή	μαθητής	νεανίας
Singular	**Nominative** (subject)	ος	ον	α	α	η	ης	ας
	Genitive/Abl (of / from)	ου	ου	ας	ης	ης	ου	ου
	Dative/Loc/Inst (to / in / by)	ῳ	ῳ	ᾳ	ῃ	ῃ	ῃ	ᾳ
	Accusative (Dir. Obj.)	ον	ον	αν	αν	ην	ην	αν
Plural	**Nominative** (subject)	οι	α	αι	αι	αι	αι	αι
	Genitive/Abl (of / from)	ων	ων	ων	ων	ων	ων	ων
	Dative/Loc/Inst (to / in / by)	οις	οις	αις	αις	αις	αις	αις
	Accusative (Dir. Obj.)	ους	α	ας	ας	ας	ας	ας

5

NOUNS OF THE FIRST DECLENSION

MULTIPLE CHOICE

Choose the best answer.

____ 1. The ending -ας occurs how many times in the first declension?

     A. one   B. three   C. five   D. seven

____ 2. Which letter is considered a "sibilant phoneme?"

     A. ε   B. σ   C. ι   D. ρ

____ 3. The feminine definite article follows the _____ paradigm.

     A. δόξα   B. ἡμέρα   C. φωνή   D. ἄνθρωπος

____ 4. The masculine definite article follows the _____ paradigm.

     A. ἄνθρωπος   B. ἡμέρα   C. τέκνον   D. φωνή

____ 5. The definite article τῆς agrees in gender, number, and case with which noun?

     A. φωνῆς   B. μαθητής   C. ἀνθρώπου   D. καρδίᾳ

____ 6. The definite article τόν agrees in gender, number, and case with which noun?

     A. ἱερά   B. δῶρον   C. τέκνου   D. ἀπόστολον

____ 7. The preposition ἀπό always takes the _____ case.

     A. nominative   B. genitive   C. dative   D. accusative

____ 8. The preposition εἰς always takes the _____ case.

     A. nominative   B. genitive   C. dative   D. accusative

____ 9. The preposition ἐκ always takes the _____ case.

     A. nominative   B. genitive   C. dative   D. accusative

____ 10. The preposition ἐν always takes the _____ case.

     A. nominative   B. genitive   C. dative   D. accusative

TRUE/FALSE

Indicate whether the statement is true or false.

____ 1. There are no masculine nouns in the first declension.

____ 2. There are no neuter nouns in the first declension.

____ 3. Prepositions are always located before their corresponding nouns.

____ 4. Greek prepositions never take more than one case.

____ 5. A definite article is required to agree with the noun that it modifies in both gender and number but not in case.

____ 6. The definite article τόν agrees in gender, number, and case with δῶρον.

____ 7. The feminine definite article is restricted to modifying only feminine nouns of the first declension.

____ 8. Rough breathing marks are found over the singular and plural nominative forms of the masculine and feminine definite articles but not over any forms of the neuter definite articles.

____ 9. The definite article ὁ agrees in gender, number, and case with all three of the following nouns: ἄνθρωπος, μαθητής, and ὁδός.

____10. All first declension nouns have identical plural endings.

SHORT ANSWER

Provide a brief answer for each question.

1. Parse οἰκίαις.

2. Parse γλῶσσαν.

3. Parse ὑποκριτῶν.

4. Parse διδαχήν.

5. Parse προφῆται.

6. Decline Μεσσίας and write the corresponding definite article for each form to the left of each form.

7. Decline εἰρήνη and write the corresponding definite article for each form to the left of each form.

8. Decline θάλασσα and write the corresponding definite article for each form to the left of each form.

9. Decline μαρτυρία and write the corresponding definite article for each form to the left of each form.

10. Decline ὁδός and write the corresponding definite article for each form to the left of each form.

GREEK to ENGLISH

Provide the English translation for each Greek sentence.

1. φέρει ἡ ἀλήθεια τοῦ θεοῦ τὴν εἰρήνην εἰς τὰς καρδίας ἀνθρώπων.

   _____

   _____

2. τὸν κύριον δοξάσουσιν ἡ διακονία τῶν μαθητῶν καὶ ἡ διδαχὴ τῶν διακονῶν.

   _____

   _____

3. οὐ σώσουσιν οἱ θεοὶ τῆς γῆς τὸν κόσμον ἀφ᾽ ἁμαρτίας.

   _____

   _____

4. λύσει ἡ ἐξουσία τοῦ Χριστοῦ τὰ τέκνα ἐπιθυμίας;

   _____

   _____

5. πέμπω τοὺς μαθητὰς ἐκ τῶν ἐκκλησιῶν.

   _____

   _____

6. διδάξετε τὰς ἀληθείας τοῦ εὐαγγελίου καὶ τοῖς νεανίαις καὶ τοῖς ἁμαρτωλοῖς τῆς γῆς.

   _____

   _____

7. ἄξεις τὸν προφήτην ἀπὸ τῆς οἰκίας ἁμαρτίας καὶ εἰς τὸ ἱερὸν τοῦ θεοῦ εἰρήνης.

   _____

   _____

8. ἔχει ὁ Μεσσίας χαρὰν ἐν τῇ ἐντολῇ τοῦ θεοῦ.

   _____

   _____

9. ζωὴν ἐκ θανάτου φέρει ὁ λόγος θεοῦ.

   _____

   _____

10. προσευχή ἐστι τὸ ἔργον τῶν τέκνων θεοῦ, ὀργὴ δέ ἐστιν ἡ ὁδὸς τῶν ὑποκριτῶν.

    _____

    _____

11. κηρύσσουσιν οἱ δοῦλοι ἐν σοφίᾳ καὶ ἀγάπῃ.

    _____

    _____

12. τοὺς ἀνθρώπους εἰς τὰς ἡμέρας δικαιοσύνης ἄγω.

    _____

    _____

13. λέγουσιν οἱ στρατιῶται τῆς βασιλείας δόξης τοὺς λόγους τοῦ Ἰησοῦ.

    _____

    _____

14. οὐ λέγουσιν αἱ γλῶσσαι τῶν τελωνῶν λόγους ζωῆς, καὶ ἡ διδαχὴ τῶν τελωνῶν οὐκ ἔστιν ἡ διδαχὴ θεοῦ.

    _____

    _____

15. βλέπει ὁ ἀπόστολος καὶ τὴν κεφαλὴν καὶ τὴν ψυχὴν τῶν ἀδελφῶν τοῦ κυρίου;

    _____

    _____

16. ἐστὶν ἡ ἀλήθεια καὶ ἐν ταῖς ἐπιστολαῖς τοῦ λόγου θεοῦ καὶ ἐν τῇ ζωῇ τοῦ υἱοῦ θεοῦ.

_____

_____

17. γινώσκετε τὴν ἡμέραν καὶ τὴν ὥραν τῆς σωτηρίας;

_____

_____

18. γράφουσιν οἱ προφῆται τὰς γραφὰς ἀλλ' οὐ γινώσκουσιν τοὺς λόγους τοῦ Ἰησοῦ ἀπὸ τῆς ἀρχῆς.

_____

_____

19. εἰρήνην καὶ ὑπομονὴν ταῖς καρδίαις ἀνθρώπων φέρουσιν αἱ διαθῆκαι θεοῦ καὶ αἱ μαρτυρίαι ἀνθρώπων.

_____

_____

20. πιστεύεις ἐν ταῖς παραβολαῖς τοῦ Ἰησοῦ;

_____

_____

21. λαμβάνει Ἰησοῦς Χριστὸς δόξαν ἀπὸ τῆς φωνῆς ἐν τῇ ἐρήμῳ.

_____

_____

22. ἀκούσουσιν οἱ μαθηταὶ τὰς προσευχὰς τοῦ ἁμαρτωλοῦ ἐν τῇ συναγωγῇ ἀλλ' οὐκ ἄξουσιν τὸν ἄνθρωπον εἰς τὴν ὁδὸν σωτηρίας.

_____

_____

23. περιτομὴ τῆς καρδίας κηρύσσει τὸ ἔργον τοῦ κυρίου.

_____

_____

24. τοὺς ὄχλους εἰς θάνατον καὶ ἁμαρτίαν ἄγει ἡ βασιλεία ἀνθρώπων.

_____

_____

25. σώσει ἡ ἀγάπη θεοῦ, φέρουσιν δὲ αἱ ἐπιθυμίαι ἀνθρώπων θάνατον.

_____

_____

26. τὰ ἱερὰ ἀνθρώπου οὐ δοξάζει τὸν θεόν, αἱ δὲ ψυχαὶ τῶν μαθητῶν οὐ βλέπουσιν θάνατον.

_____

_____

27. τὸ εὐαγγέλιον τοῖς τέκνοις ὁ διάκονος διδάσκει, ἀλλὰ τὰ τέκνα οὐκ ἔχει καρδίας χαρᾶς.

_____

_____

28. αἱ φωναὶ τῶν νεανιῶν λέγουσιν λόγους θανάτου, ἀλλ' ὁ κύριος λέγει ἀληθείας.

_____

_____

29. βλέπει ὁ κύριος δόξης καὶ τὴν γῆν καὶ τὴν θάλασσαν, ἀλλ' οἱ υἱοὶ τῆς γῆς κηρύσσουσιν τοὺς θεοὺς τοῦ κόσμου.

_____

_____

30. βαπτίζει ὁ ἀπόστολος ἐν τῇ θαλάσσῃ καὶ κηρύσσει τὴν βασιλείαν τοῦ θεοῦ ἐν παρρησίᾳ.

_____

_____

ENGLISH to GREEK

Provide the Greek translation for each English sentence.

1. The law of circumcision is in the Scriptures.

_____

_____

2. The sin of lust speaks to the hearts of young men.

_____

_____

3. We will not baptize the tax collectors in the church of God.

_____

_____

4. Do the apostles have authority from both men and God?

_____

_____

5. The angels and the children do not know the day and the hour.

_____

_____

6. You (pl.) speak truth, but they do not receive the word.

_____

_____

7. I lead the hypocrites to joy and peace.

_____

_____

8. Will the temples of the sinners lead the sons of the earth into the wrath of God?

_____

_____

9.   The voice of the Lord speaks commandments to the children.

_____

_____

10.   The man teaches from the stone in the temple.

_____

_____

11.   The disciples are sinners, but the son is truth.

_____

_____

12.   Do we baptize both the soldiers and the prophets into the kingdom of love?

_____

_____

13.   I am the way, the truth, and the life.

_____

_____

14.   The head of the church will not hear the teaching of the Messiah.

_____

_____

15.   The prophets of sinners do not know the way into the wilderness.

_____

_____

16.   The angels send the children into the ministry of the world.

_____

_____

17. The servants bring the wisdom of the earth into the synagogue of death.

_____

_____

18. Does sin take the joy of the children out of the house?

_____

_____

19. You (pl.) trust in the parables, but we believe the Lord.

_____

_____

20. The day of boldness is the hour of peace.

_____

_____

ADJECTIVES OF THE FIRST AND SECOND DECLENSIONS

MATCHING

Match each term with the most appropriate option.

_____ 1. adjective

_____ 2. three-termination adjective

_____ 3. two-termination adjective

_____ 4. compound adjective

_____ 5. attributive

_____ 6. predicate

_____ 7. substantival

_____ 8. ascriptive attributive position

_____ 9. restrictive attributive position

_____ 10. indefinite adjectival construction

A. an adjective used as a complement to the verb "to be"

B. an adjectival phrase where the English "a" or "an" is used

C. a word that describes or modifies a noun

D. an adjective used to attribute a quality to the noun it modifies

E. an adjective that uses masculine, feminine and neuter forms

F. ὁ ἄνθρωπος ὁ ἀγαθός

G. an adjective that serves as a noun

H. an adjective that uses the masculine forms for both masculine and feminine.

I. ὁ ἀγαθὸς ἄνθρωπος

J. an adjective with two or more constituent parts (e.g., ἀδύνατος or ἄπιστος)

MULTIPLE CHOICE

Choose the best answer.

____ 1. A Greek adjective must agree with its noun in _____.

    A. gender   B. number   C. case   D. all of the above

____ 2. Which of the following forms is NOT one of the nominative singular forms for the three-termination adjective ἀγαθός?

    A. ἀγαθός   B. ἀγαθά   C. ἀγαθή   D. ἀγαθόν

____ 3. Which of the following forms is NOT one of the nominative singular forms for the three-termination adjective μικρός?

    A. μικρός   B. μικρά   C. μικρή   D. μικρόν

____ 4. Endings for all three-termination feminine adjectives utilize _____ feminine endings.

    A. 1st declension   B. 2nd declension   C. both A and B   D. neither A nor B

____ 5. Endings for all three-termination neuter adjectives utilize _____ neuter endings.

    A. 1st declension   B. 2nd declension   C. both A and B   D. neither A nor B

____ 6. Endings for all three-termination masculine adjectives utilize _____ masculine endings.

    A. 1st declension   B. 2nd declension   C. both A and B   D. neither A nor B

____ 7. The adjectival construction ἡ δικαία represents the _____ position.

    A. attributive   B. predicate   C. substantival   D. nominative

____ 8. The adjectival construction ἡ δικαία διδαχή represents the _____ position.

    A. attributive   B. predicate   C. substantival   D. nominative

____ 9. The adjectival construction ἡ διδαχὴ δικαία represents the _____ position.

    A. attributive   B. predicate   C. substantival   D. nominative

____ 10. ἀγαθὸς ἄνθρωπος represents a(n) _____ construction.

    A. attributive   B. predicate   C. substantival   D. indefinite

TRUE/FALSE

Indicate whether the statement is true or false.

_____ 1. All *two-termination* adjectives are compound adjectives.

_____ 2. An adjective with a stem ending in ε, ι, ρ will follow the φωνή endings.

_____ 3. An adjective used attributively will always be located *between* the definite article and the noun.

_____ 4. An adjective used predicatively will *sometimes* be located between the definite article and the noun.

_____ 5. If the endings of both an adjective and noun agree grammatically, this means that the same endings will always agree phonetically.

_____ 6. Unlike nouns of the first and second declension, Greek adjectives of the first and second declension take iota subscripts with all dative singular forms.

_____ 7. If the stem of a three-termination feminine adjective ends in ε, ι, or ρ, the adjective will follow the ἡμέρα paradigm.

_____ 8. Two-termination adjectives are restricted to modifying only masculine and neuter words.

_____ 9. The adjectival construction ἀγαθὸς ἄνθρωπος could possibly be translated both as "a good man" and "a man is good."

_____ 10. The endings of both the adjective and the noun that it is modifying do not have to agree phonetically in order to be in grammatical agreement.

GREEK to ENGLISH

Provide the English translation for each Greek sentence.

1. οἱ πονηροὶ διδάσκουσι περιτομήν.

_____

_____

2. ὁ ἀπόστολος καλὸς καὶ ὁ προφήτης ἀγαθός.

    _____

    _____

3. αἱ ἄπιστοι ἄγουσιν τὸν ἀκάθαρτον τελώνην εἰς ἁμαρτίαν.

    _____

    _____

4. τοὺς μικροὺς εἰς ἁμαρτίαν ἄξουσιν αἱ κακαὶ γλῶσσαι τῶν πονηρῶν τέκνων.

    _____

    _____

5. ἀκούσουσιν οἱ υἱοὶ οἱ καλοὶ τὴν δικαίαν διδαχὴν ἀπὸ Ἰησοῦ Χριστοῦ.

    _____

    _____

6. ἡ ἀγαπητὴ ἐπιστολὴ διδάξει τοὺς σοφοὺς μαθητάς.

    _____

    _____

7. μικρὸν τὸ ἱερόν, ἀλλ᾽ ἡ συναγωγὴ μακαρία.

    _____

    _____

8. αἱ ἰσχυραὶ θεραπεύσουσιν τοὺς ἀξίους;

    _____

    _____

9. λέγετε καὶ τῇ ἰσχυρᾷ καὶ τῷ ἁγίῳ;

    _____

    _____

10. οὐ γινώσκεις τὴν ὁδὸν τὴν ἑτέραν εἰς τὰς οἰκίας χαρᾶς.

    _____

    _____

11. τοὺς νεκροὺς ἡ ὁδὸς ἡ αἰώνιος θεοῦ σώζει.

     _____

     _____

12. ἀγαθὰ δῶρα φέρουσιν οἱ διάκονοι οἱ σοφοὶ τῷ ἀξίῳ ἱερῷ.

     _____

     _____

13. πέμπει ὁ πρῶτος τὴν τρίτην τῇ δευτέρᾳ θαλάσσῃ.

     _____

     _____

14. ὁ δυνατὸς δοῦλός ἐστι σοφός, ἡ δὲ ἄπιστος πιστεύσει ἐν τῷ ἀγαθῷ θεῷ.

     _____

     _____

15. πιστεύσομεν ἐν τῷ μόνῳ θεῷ;

     _____

     _____

16. ἑκάστη κεφαλὴ τῶν ἐκκλησιῶν θεοῦ πιστεύει τὸν κύριον τὸν πιστόν.

     _____

     _____

17. διδάσκει ἡ ἐσχάτη διαθήκη τὴν ὁδὸν χαρᾶς καὶ εἰρήνης.

     _____

     _____

18. ἡ μαρτυρία Χριστοῦ ἀγαθὴ καὶ ὁ Ἰησοῦς σώσει τὸν ἀκάθαρτον.

     _____

     _____

19. λαμβάνετε τὰς κακὰς εἰς τὸν οἶκον τῶν πονηρῶν προφητῶν.

     _____

     _____

20. ὁ στρατιώτης ὁ δεύτερος βαπτίζει ἑκάστην.

_____

_____

21. ἡ καρδία τοῦ ἀνθρώπου ἔχει ἁγίαν ἀγάπην.

_____

_____

22. ὁ λόγος τοῦ υἱοῦ τοῦ θεοῦ λέγει τοῖς ἀνθρώποις τοῖς κακοῖς.

_____

_____

23. βλέπεις τὴν ἄπιστον, βλέπω δὲ ἕτερον ἄνθρωπον.

_____

_____

24. αἱ γραφαὶ σῴζουσιν ἁμαρτωλοὺς καὶ θεραπεύουσιν πονηρὰς καρδίας.

_____

_____

25. οἱ ἀγαπητοὶ τῆς βασιλείας θεραπεύσουσιν τὸν ἅγιον διάκονον.

_____

_____

26. ὁ νόμος περιτομῆς ἐστιν νεκρὸς νόμος.

_____

_____

27. ἡ ἐντολὴ ἡ ἰσχυρὰ τοῦ θεοῦ κηρύσσει τοῖς δικαίοις ἀγγέλοις.

_____

_____

28. οὐκ ἀκούομεν τὰς πονηράς, ἀκούσουσιν δὲ τὴν μικρὰν φωνὴν τοῦ ἁγίου.

_____

_____

29. ἡ ἡμέρα νέα, καὶ ὁ θεὸς ἀγαθός.

   _____

   _____

30. τὰ δευτέρα βλέπει ὁ ἅγιος ἀπόστολος.

   _____

   _____

31. καλὴ διδαχὴ σώσει τοὺς πονηροὺς ἁμαρτωλοὺς ἀπὸ τῆς ὁδοῦ τοῦ θανάτου.

   _____

   _____

32. εἰμὶ ἄξιος διάκονος τοῦ εὐαγγελίου, ἀλλ᾽ εἶ πονηρὸς μαθητής.

   _____

   _____

33. σώσει ὁ υἱὸς τοῦ ἀνθρώπου τοὺς κακοὺς ἀγγέλους ἀφ᾽ ἁμαρτίας;

   _____

   _____

34. τὸ τέκνον μικρόν, ἀλλ᾽ οἱ ὄχλοι ἰσχυροί.

   _____

   _____

35. λέγεις καλὰ καὶ κηρύξεις ἀπὸ καρδίας ἀγάπης.

   _____

   _____

36. οἱ προφῆται διδάσκουσι τοὺς νόμους τῶν ἁγίων γραφῶν;

   _____

   _____

37. ἀκούει ὁ υἱὸς ὁ νεκρὸς τὴν φωνὴν τοῦ Ἰησοῦ καὶ βλέπει τὴν δόξαν τοῦ μακαρίου.

   _____

   _____

38. εἰ ἡ ἄπιστος καὶ οὐκ εἰ ἀγία.

_____

_____

39. γινώσκω τοὺς λόγους τοὺς πιστοὺς τοῦ ἀγίου υἱοῦ τοῦ θεοῦ καὶ πείσομεν τοὺς δυνατοὺς λόγους θεοῦ.

_____

_____

40. βλέπει τὰ τέκνα τὰ σοφὰ θεόν, ἀλλ' ὁ ἀγαπητὸς μαθητὴς οὐ πιστεύσει τὴν δόξαν τοῦ θεοῦ.

_____

_____

ENGLISH to GREEK

Provide the Greek translation for each English sentence.

1. The works of the Lord are eternal (use the adjective predicatively).

   _____

   _____

2. New women send the powerful angels into the sea (use one adjective substantivally and the other adjective attributively).

   _____

   _____

3. The beloved apostle will write the second letter and the third letter to the churches (use both adjectives attributively).

   _____

   _____

4. The young men will not lead the unbelieving women (use the adjective substantivally).

   _____

   _____

5. Do we hear the evil voices (use the adjective attributively)?

   _____

   _____

6. The anger is strong, but the love is eternal (use both adjectives predicatively).

   _____

   _____

7. I will preach to the small synagogue in the bad wilderness (use both adjectives attributively).

   _____

   _____

8. The God of good things receives the first glory (use one adjective substantivally and the other adjective attributively).

   _____

   _____

9. The joy of the Lord is good, and the love of Christ is eternal (use both adjectives predicatively).

   _____

   _____

10. Will the holy one of God teach in the righteous temple of man (use one adjective substantivally and the other adjective attributively)?

   _____

   _____

7

IMPERFECT AND
AORIST ACTIVE INDICATIVE

MATCHING

Choose the best answer.

_____ 1. κ, γ, χ + σ =

A. continuous action in the past (e.g., "I kept loosing")

_____ 2. π, β, φ + σ =

B. ἤγαγον (from ἄγω)

_____ 3. τ, δ, θ + σ =

C. ἤκουον (from ἀκούω)

_____ 4. process morpheme (temporal augment)

D. εἶχον (from ἔχω)

_____ 5. zero morpheme augment

E. the internal vowel change which occurs between imperfect and 2nd aorist forms (cf. English *sing, sang, sung*)

_____ 6. double augment

F. σ

_____ 7. irregular augment

G. ψ

_____ 8. vowel gradation

H. εὑρίσκετο (from εὑρίσκω)

_____ 9. progressive imperfect

I. ξ

_____ 10. customary imperfect

J. habitual action in the past (e.g., "I used to loose")

MULTIPLE CHOICE
Choose the best answer.

___ 1. Greek verbs have _____ sets of forms for indicative action in past time.

    A. two   B. three   C. four   D. five

___ 2. The aoristic aspect morpheme is represented by _____.

    A. σα   B. ε   C. ες   D. none of the above

___ 3. The only difference between imperfect and second aorist forms is the verb's _____.

    A. augment   B. suffix   C. stem   D. connecting vowel

___ 4. The original stem of a Greek verb is often preserved in the _____ stem.

    A. imperfect   B. 1st aorist   C. 2nd aorist   D. none of the above

___ 5. In the Greek word ἐλύετο, the letters λυ represent the _____.

    A. lexical morpheme   B. past time morpheme   C. person-number suffix   D. neutral morpheme

___ 6. In the Greek word ἐλύετο, the letters το represent the _____.

    A. lexical morpheme   B. past time morpheme   C. person-number suffix   D. neutral morpheme

___ 7. In the Greek word ἐλύετο, the first ε represents the _____.

    A. lexical morpheme   B. past time morpheme   C. person-number suffix   D. neutral morpheme

___ 8. In the Greek word ἐλύετο, the second ε represents the _____.

    A. lexical morpheme   B. past time morpheme   C. person-number suffix   D. neutral morpheme

___ 9. In the Greek word ἔλυσαν, the letters σα represent the _____.

    A. aoristic aspect morpheme   B. past time morpheme   C. case-number suffix   D. neutral morpheme

___10. The translation for the Greek word ἐθεράπευον is

    A. "they heal"   B. "they healed"   C. "they were healing"   D. "they have healed"

TRUE/FALSE

Indicate whether the statement is true or false.

____ 1. *Kind* of action can also be referred to as "verbal aspect."

____ 2. The majority of Greek verbs have both first and second aorist forms.

____ 3. First aorist and second aorist verbs are different in form but not function.

____ 4. The verb εὕρισκον could possibly be translated both as "he/she/it was finding" and "they found."

____ 5. The imperfect forms of εἰμί have smooth breathing marks.

____ 6. There is no difference in meaning between the second aorist form of the verb "we sinned" (ἡμάρτομεν) and the first aorist form of the verb "we sinned" (ἡμαρτήσαμεν).

____ 7. The rules of linguistics do not allow Greek verbs to substitute entirely different forms for their second aorist forms.

____ 8. The imperfect form of a particular Greek verb is identical to its second aorist form except for its stem.

____ 9. Amalgamation will always occur when creating any first aorist verb form.

____ 10. Amalgamation only occurs in the creation of the future tense form of Greek verbs.

GREEK to ENGLISH

Provide the English translation for each Greek sentence.

1. ὁ μαθητὴς ἦν ἀγαθός, οὐ δὲ εἶδεν τὴν μακαρίαν δόξαν τοῦ θεοῦ.

   _____

   _____

2. αἱ ἄπιστοι οὐχ ἡτοίμασαν τὴν ὁδὸν τοῦ κυρίου.

   _____

   _____

3. ἔβλεψεν τὰς ἰσχυρᾶς ἐν τῇ συναγωγῇ, ἀλλ᾽ ἐδίδαξαν ἕτερον εὐαγγέλιον.

   _____

   _____

4. ἔλυεν ὁ πονηρὸς τοὺς ἀγγέλους θανάτου, καὶ οὐκ ἔλιπον τοὺς θεοὺς τῆς γῆς.

   _____

   _____

5. ἔμαθεν ὁ πιστὸς ἀπόστολος τὰς ὁδοὺς τῆς ἀγαθῆς ζωῆς.

   _____

   _____

6. ἔσχες εἰρήνην ἐν τῇ ἐκκλησίᾳ, ἀλλ᾽ ἔχεις ὀργὴν ἐν τῷ οἴκῳ.

   _____

   _____

7. ἔπεισεν ὁ προφήτης τὴν διαθήκην τὴν καινὴν καὶ ἔλαβεν σωτηρίαν ἀπὸ τοῦ κυρίου.

   _____

   _____

8. εὕρετε τοὺς λίθους ἀπὸ τῆς θαλάσσης, ἐβάλομεν δὲ τοὺς λίθους εἰς τὸ ἱερόν.

   _____

   _____

9. οὐκ ἔπασχον κακὰ ἀπὸ τῶν ὑποκριτῶν, ἀλλ᾽ ἔφυγον τοῖς οἴκοις τοῦ ἀγαπητοῦ ἀποστόλου.

    _____

    _____

10. ὁ ἀπόστολος ἐθεράπευσεν τοὺς ὄχλους τοὺς δικαίους, ἀλλ᾽ οὐκ ἔγνων τοὺς ἀποστόλους.

    _____

    _____

11. ἤνεγκεν ὁ Χριστὸς τὰς ἁμαρτίας τοῦ κόσμου καὶ ἤγαγεν ἁμαρτωλοὺς ἀπὸ ζωῆς ἐν ἁμαρτίᾳ.

    _____

    _____

12. ἔμαθον τὰς ἀληθείας τοῦ θεοῦ, καὶ ἐκηρύξαμεν ἐν τῷ ἱερῷ.

    _____

    _____

13. ἔλαβες τὰ δῶρα ἀπὸ τῶν μικρῶν τέκνων;

    _____

    _____

14. εἶδες τὸν υἱὸν τοῦ ἀνθρώπου; βλέψετε τὸν Χριστόν;

    _____

    _____

15. ἔλιπεν ὁ στρατιώτης τὸ ἱερόν, ὁ δὲ μαθητὴς ἔπεμψαν αὐτὸν εἰς τὴν συναγωγήν.

    _____

    _____

16. ἠκούσατε τὰς φωνὰς τῶν δούλων τῶν δικαίων, ἀλλ᾽ οὐκ ἐκήρυσσον ἐν τῇ ἐρήμῳ.

    _____

    _____

17. ἔφυγον οἱ υἱοὶ οἱ καλοὶ ἐκ τῶν ἐκκλησιῶν καὶ ἡτοίμασαν τὴν ὁδὸν τοῦ κυρίου.

_____

_____

18. ἡ καρδία πονηρά, ἐδόξασεν δὲ ἡ κεφαλὴ τῆς ἐκκλησίας τὸν θεόν.

_____

_____

19. ἐκήρυσσον εἰς τὴν ἀρχὴν τῆς τρίτης ἡμέρας.

_____

_____

20. εὑρίσκει ὁ ἄξιος σωτηρίαν καὶ εἰρήνην, εὕρομεν δὲ θάνατον.

_____

_____

21. ἥμαρτον οἱ ἁμαρτωλοὶ τὰς ἁμαρτίας, ἀλλ᾽ ἦγεν τοὺς ἀνθρώπους τῆς γῆς τῇ φωνῇ τοῦ θεοῦ.

_____

_____

22. ἐβάπτιζεν ὁ δίκαιος διάκονος τοὺς δυνατοὺς ὄχλους τῶν στρατιωτῶν.

_____

_____

23. εἶπεν τὸ μικρὸν τέκνον τὰς γραφὰς τοῖς ἀνθρώποις.

_____

_____

24. ἐμάθετε, ἔγραψας, καὶ εὕρομεν τὴν ἀλήθειαν.

_____

_____

25. ἐδίδαξαν αἱ ἅγιαι παραβολαὶ ζωὴν αἰώνιον;

_____

_____

26. ἡτοίμασας τὴν ὁδὸν τοῦ κυρίου καὶ ἐδόξασα τὸν θεόν.

_____

_____

27. ἐδίδασκον οἱ καινοὶ τὰ τέκνα ἐν ταῖς οἰκίαις, ἀλλ' οἱ ἰσχυροὶ ἔπαθον ἐν τῇ ἐρήμῳ.

_____

28. ἤμην ἁμαρτωλός, ἦς δὲ μαθητὴς Χριστοῦ.

_____

_____

29. εἶδεν τὴν βασιλείαν τοῦ κυρίου, ἀλλ' ἔλιπεν τὸν οἶκον καὶ ἐδίδαξεν πονηρὰν διδαχήν.

_____

_____

30. βλέπει ὁ ἀγαθὸς προφήτης τὸ ἱερόν, καὶ μανθάνομεν ἀπὸ Ἰησοῦ ἐν τῇ συναγωγῇ.

_____

_____

31. ἐμάνθανε τὴν ὁδὸν τῆς εἰρήνης καὶ ἀληθείας, ἀλλ' ἔφυγον ἀπὸ τοῦ μαθητοῦ.

_____

_____

32. ἔσωζεν ὁ υἱὸς τοῦ θεοῦ ἀνθρώπους, ἤμην δὲ ἐν τῷ ἑτέρῳ οἴκῳ.

_____

_____

33. ἑκάστη ἐντολὴ θεοῦ ἔσωσεν τὰς καρδίας τὰς πιστὰς τοῦ κόσμου.

_____

_____

34. ἔγνωμεν τὴν διακονίαν τοῦ Ἰησοῦ Χριστοῦ;

_____

_____

35. ἦς μακαρία καὶ ἤμην ἀγαπητός, ἀλλ᾽ ἦν πονηρά.

_____

_____

36. ἔβαλον οἱ ἄγγελοι τοὺς ἄλλους ἀνθρώπους ἐκ τοῦ ἱεροῦ καὶ εἰς τὴν κακὴν ἔρημον.

_____

_____

37. ἐθεράπευσεν ὁ Μεσσίας τὰς ζωὰς τῶν νεκρῶν νεανιῶν καὶ ἐκήρυξεν τὴν δόξαν τοῦ θεοῦ.

_____

_____

38. οἱ μαθηταὶ ἔπαθον, καὶ ἔφυγες εἰς τὴν ὁδὸν ἁμαρτίας.

_____

_____

39. ἠγάγετε τὸν μόνον υἱὸν εἰς τὴν ἐκκλησίαν, ἦγον δὲ τοὺς δούλους ἐκ τῆς ἐρήμου.

_____

_____

40. ἔπεμψαν τὸν Χριστὸν ἐκ τῆς συναγωγῆς καὶ εἶπον πονηρὰ τῷ Πέτρῳ.

_____

_____

ENGLISH to GREEK

Provide the Greek translation for each English sentence.

1. He bore the sins of the world.

_____

_____

2.   I saw and received the gifts from the children.

_____

_____

3.   The worthy apostle glorified the road to salvation.

_____

_____

4.   Did the wise teachings save the men from sin and death?

_____

_____

5.   We were the first children of the strong prophet.

_____

_____

6.   They did not baptize in the way of life.

_____

_____

7.   You (sg.) were leaving the house, but you (pl.) left the churches.

_____

_____

8.   You were powerful apostles, but He was the Son of God.

_____

_____

9.   The ministers wrote the words of truth, but the disciples fled from the words of God.

_____

_____

10.   Were the young men leaving the temple?

_____

_____

ADDITIONAL PREPOSITIONS

Place the correct translation for the following two- and three-case prepositions within the appropriate boxes. Place an "X" in the box if the preposition is NOT used with that particular case.

PREPOSITION	GENITIVE	DATIVE	ACCUSATIVE
διά			
κατά			
μετά			
περί			
ὑπέρ			
ὑπό			
ἐπί			
παρά			
ἀνά			
ἀντί			
πρό			
πρός			
σύν			

GREEK to ENGLISH

Provide the English translation for each Greek sentence.

1. ἔφυγεν διὰ τῆς ἐρήμου διὰ τὴν ὀργὴν τοῦ πονηροῦ ἀγγέλου.

   _____

   _____

2. ἀναγινώσκετε τὰς γραφὰς κατὰ τὴν ἐντολὴν τοῦ Χριστοῦ.

   _____

   _____

3. ἀπέθνῃσκεν μετὰ ἀγαθῆς μαρτυρίας, καὶ οἱ μαθηταὶ ἀπέθανον μετὰ τὸν θάνατον τοῦ Χριστοῦ.

   _____

   _____

4. περὶ τὴν θάλασσαν ὁ προφήτης ἐκήρυξεν τὸ εὐαγγέλιον ἀνθρώποις.

   _____

   _____

5. ἦμεν ὑπὸ τὸν νόμον διὰ τὴν διδαχὴν τῶν συναγωγῶν.

   _____

   _____

6. ὁ τελώνης ἀνοίγει τὰ ἱερὰ καὶ κηρύσσει κατὰ τῆς ἐξουσίας τοῦ Χριστοῦ.

   _____

   _____

7. βαπτίσει ὁ νεανίας ὑπὲρ τῆς δόξης τοῦ κυρίου, ἀλλ᾽ ὁ πονηρὸς προφήτης ἐξέβαλεν τὸν νεανίαν ἐκ τοῦ ἱεροῦ.

   _____

   _____

8. ὁ Χριστὸς ἔλιπεν τὴν δόξαν τῆς βασιλείας καὶ ἀπέθανεν κακὸν θάνατον.

   _____

   _____

9. ἤκουσεν ὁ νεὸς υἱὸς περὶ εἰρήνης ἀντὶ πονηρῶν ἐντολῶν.

   _____

   _____

10. εἴδομεν τὸν ἄγγελον παρὰ τὸ ἱερόν, ἀλλ᾽ οὐκ ἤμην σὺν τῷ ἀγγέλῳ.

    _____

    _____

11. ἔγραφεν ὁ θεὸς τοὺς λόγους ἐπὶ ταῖς καρδίαις τοῦ ὄχλου.

    _____

    _____

12. πέμψει ὁ θεὸς τοὺς δυνατοὺς στρατιώτας κατὰ τὰς γραφάς.

    _____

    _____

13. οἱ διάκονοι ἔχουσιν τὴν χαρὰν τοῦ κυρίου ἀντὶ τῆς ὀργῆς τοῦ ἀνθρώπου.

    _____

    _____

14. ἔσωσεν ὁ υἱὸς τοῦ θεοῦ τὸν νεκρὸν πρὸ τῆς ἀρχῆς τοῦ κόσμου.

    _____

    _____

15. βλέψετε τὴν ἀλήθειαν διὰ τὴν ἐξουσίαν τῶν γραφῶν.

    _____

    _____

16. διδάσκεις παρὰ τὸ ἱερὸν σὺν καρδίᾳ ὀργῆς;

    _____

    _____

17. ἀπέθανεν ἡ διαθήκη ἡ τρίτη, ἀλλ᾽ ὁ ἀπόστολος ἐδίδασκεν τὴν ἀλήθειαν περὶ τοῦ ἁγίου περὶ τὴν θάλασσαν.

    _____

    _____

18. ἡ γῆ λέγει περὶ τῶν δοξῶν τοῦ θεοῦ κατὰ τὰς γραφάς.

_____

_____

19. ἤγαγον τοὺς ὄχλους εἰς τὸ ἅγιον ἱερὸν καὶ ἐδίδαξα τὰς ἐντολὰς τῆς βασιλείας.

_____

_____

20. ὁ Ἰησοῦς ἔβλεψεν τὸν ὄχλον καὶ ἔλιπεν σὺν τοῖς υἱοῖς τῶν ἀνθρώπων.

_____

_____

21. ἄγει ὁ κακὸς ἄγγελος τοὺς στρατιώτας παρὰ τῶν ἡμερῶν τῆς σωτηρίας.

_____

_____

22. καὶ ὁ μαθητὴς καὶ οἱ προφῆται ἐκήρυξαν περὶ τῶν νεῶν προσευχῶν ἀγάπης.

_____

_____

23. λέγει κατὰ τὸν νόμον, ὁ δὲ Χριστὸς ἔχει ἀγάπην ὑπὲρ ἑκάστου ἀνθρώπου.

_____

_____

24. ἤμην ὑπὸ τὴν γῆν, ἦς δὲ ὑπὲρ τὸν κόσμον μετὰ τῶν ἀγγέλων.

_____

_____

25. λέγουσιν κατὰ τὴν ἐπιστολὴν τοῦ νόμου, ἀλλ' ὁ θεὸς γράφει νόμον ἐπὶ ταῖς καρδίαις τῶν ἀνθρώπων.

_____

_____

26. οὐκ ἔγνων τὴν ἀγάπην τοῦ προφήτου ἀντὶ τῆς ὀργῆς τῆς ἀπίστου;

_____

_____

27. περὶ τὴν ἐκκλησίαν ἐκηρύξαμεν περὶ τοῦ δούλου τοῦ ἀκαθάρτου καὶ κατὰ τῆς πονηρᾶς.

_____

_____

28. ἐν ἀρχῇ ἐλάβομεν τὸ εὐαγγέλιον παρὰ τὴν θάλασσαν.

_____

_____

29. ὁ μακάριος ἀπόστολος καὶ ὁ πρῶτος νεανίας εὗρον τὰ τέκνα μετὰ τὰς πιστάς.

_____

_____

30. ἦσαν κατὰ τῆς ἐξουσίας τῶν ὑποκριτῶν, ἀλλ᾽ ἦτε ὑπὲρ τὸν νόμον.

_____

_____

31. ἐλάμβανεν ὁ ἰσχυρὸς τοὺς πονηροὺς διακόνους μετὰ καρδιῶν λίθου.

_____

_____

32. κηρύσσουσιν κατὰ τὴν ἐντολὴν τῶν ἁγίων γραφῶν.

_____

_____

33. ἐδίδασκον τὰ τέκνα τοῦ ἱεροῦ καὶ οἱ διάκονοι τοῦ εὐαγγελίου περὶ τῶν γλωσσῶν τῶν ἀνθρώπων;

_____

_____

34. ὁ υἱὸς τοῦ θεοῦ ἀνοίγει τὰς γραφὰς καὶ διδάσκει περὶ τῶν λόγων τῆς ζωῆς.

_____

_____

35. λέγομεν παρὰ γλώσσαις ἀνθρώπων καὶ ἀγγέλων παρὰ τὴν θάλασσαν.

_____

_____

36. ἔφερεν τὸ ἔργον τοῦ μαθητοῦ λόγους ζωῆς τῷ ὄχλῳ ἀντὶ θανάτου.

_____

_____

37. ἑτοιμάσει ἡ ἀγάπη τοῦ Χριστοῦ τὴν ἀλήθειαν ὑπὲρ τοῦ κόσμου.

_____

_____

38. ὁ νόμος τῶν προφητῶν ἐστιν ἐν ταῖς κεφαλαῖς τῶν ἀποστόλων.

_____

_____

39. ἦν ὁ λόγος ἄνθρωπος, καὶ ἦν ὁ λόγος σὺν ἀνθρώπῳ.

_____

_____

40. ἔσῳζεν ὁ Μεσσίας ὁ μακάριος τοὺς πονηροὺς ἀγγέλους ἀπὸ θανάτου.

_____

_____

ENGLISH to GREEK

Provide the Greek translation for each English sentence.

1. They received the circumcision upon the heart.

_____

_____

2. The good laws of the earth were teaching the children about the hour of salvation.

   _____

   _____

3. The voice of the crowd said to the hypocrites, "The Lord is with man."

   _____

   _____

4. The evil men and the little children prepared the gods of stone under the earth.

   _____

   _____

5. Were you (pl.) baptizing according to the authority of the Scriptures?

   _____

   _____

6. Tax collectors and sinners were bearing gifts to the Christ instead of sins.

   _____

   _____

7. You (sg.) did not see the covenant of stone around the sea.

   _____

   _____

8. They know the peace of Christ, but I do not know the way of truth.

   _____

   _____

9. The ministers did not teach about Christ with boldness according to the Scriptures.

   _____

   _____

10. The letters bring eternal life into the world instead of death.

   _____

   _____

9

PERSONAL PRONOUNS

MATCHING

Match each term with the most appropriate option.

___ 1. ἐμέ	A.	enclitic form of "me"
___ 2. με	B.	"him"
___ 3. antecedent	C.	"self"
___ 4. adjectival αὐτός	D.	emphatic form of "me"
___ 5. intensive αὐτός	E.	noun for which a pronoun stands
___ 6. αὐτό	F.	"you"
___ 7. αὐτόν	G.	"same"
___ 8. ὑμεῖς	H.	"we"
___ 9. ἡμεῖς	I.	"of them, their"
___ 10. αὐτῶν	J.	"it"

MULTIPLE CHOICE

Choose the best answer.

___ 1. A personal pronoun must agree with its antecedent in the following ways:

    A. gender only   B. gender and number only   C. gender, number, and case only

___ 2. There are _____ classes of pronouns in the New Testament.

    A. five   B. eight   C. nine   D. ten

___ 3. Pronouns can be used in place of nouns to avoid _____.

    A. word repetition   B. monotony   C. redundancy   D. all of the above

___ 4. Personal pronouns in the _____ case are frequently used to express possession.

    A. nominative   B. genitive   C. dative   D. accusative

___ 5. The emphatic forms of the personal pronoun are normally used after _____.

    A. prepositions   B. nouns   C. adjectives   D. verbs

___ 6. The noun for which a pronoun stands is called an _____.

    A. amalgamation   B. enclitic   C. antecedent   D. allomorph

___ 7. Personal pronouns are used in the _____ case only when emphasis is needed.

    A. nominative   B. genitive   C. dative   D. accusative

___ 8. If the personal pronoun αὐτόν immediately follows the preposition "κατά," the Greek construction will be

    A. κατὰ αὐτόν   B. κατ' αὐτόν   C. καθ' αὐτόν   D. κατὰ αὐτό

___ 9. The third person personal pronoun αὐτής can be translated either "of her" or

    A. "hers"   B. "her"   C. "her's"   D. none of the above

___10. ὁ κύριος αὐτὸς λέγει should be translated as

    A. "The Lord He speaks"   B. "The Lord Himself speaks"   C. "The same Lord speaks"

TRUE/FALSE

Choose whether the statement is true or false.

____ 1. A Greek pronoun must agree with its antecedent in gender, number, and case.

____ 2. Personal pronouns are used in the *dative* case only when emphasis is intended.

____ 3. The English word *pronoun* is derived from two Latin words *pro* and *nomen* which means "use along with a noun."

____ 4. με and ἐμέ are both translated as "me" (in English) but are not equal in emphasis.

____ 5. Plural forms of personal pronouns do not have enclitic forms.

____ 6. The declension of αὐτός, αὐτή, αὐτό is identical to that of the adjective καλός without exception.

____ 7. All personal pronouns take smooth breathing marks.

____ 8. Personal pronouns do not take iota subscripts in their dative singular forms.

____ 9. The neuter, singular, accusative, personal pronoun form ends in a ν.

____10. There are no vocative forms for third person personal pronouns.

GREEK to ENGLISH

Provide the English translation for each Greek sentence.

1. ἡμεῖς ἠκούσαμεν τοὺς αὐτοὺς λόγους ἀλλ' οὐκ ἐπιστεύσαμεν αὐτούς.

_____

_____

2. τὸ ἱερόν μου ἔλαβεν τοὺς δούλους παρὰ τῶν πονηρῶν οἴκων ὑμῶν.

_____

_____

3. γινώσκεις ἡμᾶς καὶ ἡμεῖς ἀκούομεν ὑμᾶς, ὑμεῖς δὲ οὐ βλέπετε αὐτούς.

_____

_____

4. σὺ κηρύξεις τὰς σοφὰς ἀληθείας τοῦ θεοῦ ἡμῶν τοῖς υἱοῖς ὑμῶν.

_____

_____

5. ὁ κύριος αὐτὸς ἀκούσει τοὺς λόγους μου, καὶ αὐτὸς θεραπεύσει τὴν γῆν ἡμῶν.

_____

_____

6. καθ᾽ ἡμέραν ἡ προσευχή μου ἐθεράπευεν τοὺς νεανίας.

_____

_____

7. ὁ διάκονος ὁ δίκαιός μου ἔλιπεν τὸ κακὸν ἱερόν σου.

_____

_____

8. οἱ τελῶναι ἐδίδασκον ἡμᾶς περὶ σοφίας καὶ χαρᾶς καὶ σωτηρίας.

_____

_____

9. οἱ μαθηταὶ αὐτῆς οὐ λύουσιν τὰς ἁμαρτίας ὑμῶν ἀπὸ τῆς βασιλείας τοῦ θανάτου.

_____

_____

10. ἡμεῖς ἀπεθάνομεν μετὰ ὀργῆς διὰ τὴν ἄπιστον ἀγάπην σου.

_____

_____

11. οἱ ἄγγελοι αὐτοὶ ἐδόξαζον τὸν θεὸν αὐτῶν ἐν τῇ οἰκίᾳ αὐτῆς.

_____

_____

12. σὺ εἶ ἀπόστολος, ἐγὼ δέ εἰμι ὁ υἱὸς ὁ πονηρὸς τοῦ θανάτου.

_____

_____

13. ὁ Μεσσίας εὗρεν τὴν διαθήκην αὐτοῦ ἐν ταῖς καρδίαις τῶν τέκνων αὐτοῦ.

_____

_____

14. ὁ προφήτης ἔγραψεν τὴν παραβολὴν ὑμῖν κατὰ τὴν ἐντολὴν τοῦ θεοῦ μου.

_____

_____

15. ἡτοίμασάν σε ὑπὲρ τῆς ἐξουσίας τοῦ θεοῦ, ἀλλ' ὁ αὐτὸς θεὸς ἐξέβαλεν τοὺς κακοὺς ἐκ τῶν ἱερῶν.

_____

_____

16. οἱ λόγοι σου ἔπεμψεν τοὺς αὐτοὺς στρατιώτας εἰς τὸν οἶκον ἐμοῦ.

_____

_____

17. ἡ ψυχὴ αὐτῆς ἔσχεν τὴν χαρὰν τοῦ κυρίου αὐτῆς.

_____

_____

18. αὐτοὶ ἐδίδασκον τὰς ἁγίας γραφὰς τῷ δικαίῳ υἱῷ σου.

_____

_____

19. αἱ μαρτυρίαι ἡμῶν ἑτοιμάζουσιν τὸν ἄξιον ἄνθρωπον ὑπὲρ διακονίας.

_____

_____

20. ὑμεῖς ἐκβάλλετε τοὺς κακοὺς ἀνθρώπους αὐτῶν διὰ τὴν δόξαν τοῦ Χριστοῦ.

_____

_____

21. ἐγὼ ἔλεγον τὴν διδαχὴν τοῦ Χριστοῦ αὐταῖς.

_____

_____

22. ἡ αὐτὴ ἦγεν ἡμᾶς τῇ γῇ.

_____

_____

23. οἱ δίκαιοι ἡμῶν διδάσκουσι τοὺς ὄχλους περὶ περιτομῆς καὶ τῆς διαθήκης.

_____

_____

24. ἐγὼ ἔφυγον ἐκ τοῦ οἴκου καὶ εἰς τὸν ἀγρόν σου.

_____

_____

25. φέρετε τὴν ἀλήθειαν τοῦ εὐαγγελίου ὑμῖν, φέρει δὲ τὸν νόμον τοῦ ἀνθρώπου ἡμῖν.

_____

_____

26. αἱ πονηραὶ τῆς ὀργῆς ἄξουσιν ἡμᾶς εἰς τὴν ὁδὸν τῆς ἁμαρτίας, ἀλλ᾽ Ἰησοῦς θεραπεύσει αὐτὰς ἀπὸ τῶν ἁμαρτιῶν αὐτῶν.

_____

_____

27. ὑμεῖς πιστεύσετε ἐν Χριστῷ πρὸ τῶν ἀδελφῶν ὑμῶν.

_____

_____

28. ὁ ἄνθρωπος θεραπεύσει τὴν ζωὴν αὐτῆς ἀντὶ τῶν ζώων αὐτῶν.

_____

_____

29. αὐτὴ ἔχει καλὴν φωνήν, ἀλλ᾽ ὁ ὄχλος οὐκ ἀκούσουσιν αὐτήν.

_____

_____

30. λέγομεν τοὺς λόγους τῆς εἰρήνης αὐτῷ διὰ τὴν ἐντολὴν τοῦ κυρίου.

_____

_____

31. ὁ θεὸς αὐτὸς σώσει τὰς πονηρὰς ἀπὸ τῶν ἁμαρτιῶν αὐτῶν.

_____

_____

32. ἐγώ εἰμι ὁ υἱὸς τοῦ θεοῦ, καὶ ἐγὼ σώσω τὰ τέκνα τοῦ κόσμου.

_____

_____

33. αὐτὴ λέγει τοὺς λόγους ζωῆς μοι, ἀλλ᾽ ἐγὼ οὐκ ἀκούω αὐτήν.

_____

_____

34. οὐ δοξάσουσιν αἱ γλῶσσαι τῶν ἀνθρώπων τοὺς θεοὺς τοῦ λίθου αὐτῶν, δοξάσομεν δὲ θεὸν ἡμῶν.

_____

_____

35. ἡ καρδία σου οὐκ ἔστι νεκρά, ἀλλ᾽ ἡ ζωή μου οὐχ ἔξει εἰρήνην.

_____

_____

36. τὰ δῶρα τῆς ἀγάπης μου ἑτοιμάσει τοὺς δούλους ὑπὲρ τοῦ ἔργου αὐτῶν.

_____

_____

37. αἱ ὁδοὶ τοῦ κυρίου ἡμῶν εἰσιν ἀγαθαὶ καὶ σοφαί.

_____

_____

38. εὑρίσκετε ὑμεῖς τὸν οἶκον αὐτῶν διὰ τὸν πονηρὸν ἄγγελον αὐτῶν.

_____

_____

39. διδάσκουσιν αἱ παραβολαὶ καὶ ἡ διδαχὴ τοῦ ἀδελφοῦ σου τὴν ὁδὸν εἰρήνης.

_____

_____

40. ὁ λόγος τοῦ θεοῦ ἐστι πιστὸς καὶ διδάσκει καρδίας ὑπὲρ σωτηρίας.

_____

_____

ENGLISH to GREEK

Provide the Greek translation for each English sentence. Translate all English pronouns with Greek pronouns.

1. You (sg.) hear us, we know you (pl.), but I do not see them.

_____

_____

2. Our brothers were preaching their words of life to you (sg.).

_____

_____

3. The man himself was the same apostle.

_____

_____

4. My heart trusts in the glory of our Lord, and my life has your (pl.) peace.

_____

_____

5. Will you teach me about the ways of your (sg.) God?

    _____

    _____

6. The teaching of unclean young men will not save you (pl.) and me.

    _____

    _____

7. I teach the Scriptures to them about the beautiful words of Jesus, but they will not glorify Him.

    _____

    _____

8. Every work of salvation prepares you (sg.) for the kingdom of my Christ.

    _____

    _____

9. You (pl.) sinned in the house, but you (pl.) are saving the children of our apostles.

    _____

    _____

10. We fled from the death of sinners and hypocrites because of my sons.

    _____

    _____

PERFECT AND PLUPERFECT ACTIVE INDICATIVE

MATCHING

Choose the best answer.

____ 1. γέγραφα

____ 2. λέλυκα

____ 3. τ

____ 4. π

____ 5. ἐπεποίθεισαν

____ 6. ἀκηκόατε

____ 7. κα

____ 8. οἶδα

____ 9. οἴδατε

____ 10. ἤδειτε

A. the corresponding unaspirated consonant of θ

B. "you have heard"

C. a synonym of γινώσκω

D. a 1st perfect verb form

E. "you know"

F. a 2nd perfect verb form

G. the corresponding unaspirated consonant of φ

H. "they had trusted in"

I. "you were knowing"

J. perfective aspect morpheme

MULTIPLE CHOICE

Choose the best answer.

___ 1. In the Greek word πεπιστεύκεισαν, the letters πιστευ represent the _____.

    A. lexical morpheme   B. perfective aspect morpheme   C. reduplication   D. secondary active suffix

___ 2. In the Greek word πεπιστεύκεισαν, the letters σαν represent the _____.

    A. lexical morpheme   B. perfective aspect morpheme   C. reduplication   D. secondary active suffix

___ 3. In the Greek word πεπιστεύκεισαν, the letters πε represent the _____.

    A. lexical morpheme   B. perfective aspect morpheme   C. reduplication   D. secondary active suffix

___ 4. In the Greek word πεπιστεύκεισαν, the letters κει represent the _____.

    A. lexical morpheme   B. perfective aspect morpheme   C. reduplication   D. secondary active suffix

___ 5. The Greek word ἀκηκόει, is best translated as

    A. "he will have been heard"   B. "he has heard"   C. "he had heard"   D. "he has had heard"

___ 6. The corresponding unaspirated consonant of φ is

    A. τ   B. π   C. χ   D. ψ

___ 7. The corresponding unaspirated consonant of θ is

    A. τ   B. π   C. χ   D. ψ

___ 8. An example of a Greek verb that has experienced reduplication with a temporal augment is

    A. ἐγνώκαμεν   B. μεμάθηκεν   C. γέγραφα   D. ἡτοιμάκαμεν

___ 9. Second perfects drop the _____ within the perfective aspect morpheme.

    A. α   B. σ   C. κ   D. ε

___10. Which one of the following verbs does not take second perfect forms?

    A. γινώσκω   B. ἀκούω   C. γράφω   D. πέμπω

TRUE/FALSE

Choose whether the statement is true or false.

___ 1. The perfect tense usually refers to the present results of a past, yet incomplete, action.

___ 2. The pluperfect represents the future tense of the perfect.

___ 3. In its technical form, the pluperfect contains an augment as well as reduplication.

___ 4. οἶδα, when taking a perfect tense form, is translated as a present tense verb.

___ 5. οἶδα, when taking a pluperfect tense form, is translated as an imperfect tense verb.

___ 6. The phonemes τ, δ, or θ are dropped before the κ of the perfect.

___ 7. In its technical form, the perfect tense contains an augment that is often left off of the word in the Greek New Testament.

___ 8. The reduplication of γν is γε (as in γέγνωκα).

___ 9. The reduplication of θ is τε (as in τεθεράπευκα).

___ 10. The reduplication of ε is εε (as in ἔεετοιμακα).

GREEK to ENGLISH

Provide the English translation for each Greek sentence.

1. ἡμεῖς οἴδαμεν τὴν εἰρήνην τῆς ἀγαθῆς ζωῆς.

   _____

   _____

2. βέβληται ὁ ἀπόστολος ὁ ἅγιος τὸν καλὸν ἐκ τοῦ δικαίου ἱεροῦ.

   _____

   _____

3. αὐτοὶ ἡτοιμάκαμεν τοὺς νεοὺς οἴκους ὑπὲρ σοῦ ὅτι σὺ σέσωκας τὰ τέκνα ἡμῶν.

   _____

   _____

4. ᾔδεισαν καὶ οἱ μαθηταὶ καὶ οἱ προφῆται τοὺς πονηροὺς ὄχλους καὶ τὰς ὁδοὺς τοῦ θανάτου αὐτῶν.

   _____

   _____

5. οἶδάς με καὶ γινώσκω σε, ὑμεῖς δὲ ἡμαρτήκατε εἰς τὴν ὁδὸν τοῦ κυρίου καὶ εἰς τὰς ἐντολὰς τοῦ κυρίου ἡμῶν.

   _____

   _____

6. πεπίστευκα ὅτι ἔσχηκα σωτηρίαν μου, ἀλλ᾽ ἐγὼ οὐκ ἔσχον αὐτήν.

   _____

   _____

7. ἔγνωκεν ὁ νεανίας τὴν διδαχὴν τῆς ἀληθείας, καὶ ἔγνωκα τὸ δῶρον τῆς σωτηρίας.

   _____

   _____

8. μεμάθηκεν Φίλιππος τοὺς λόγους τῶν γραφῶν, ἀλλ᾽ ἔγνωκας τὸν λόγον ἐν τῇ καρδίᾳ σου.

   _____

   _____

9. εὕρηκας ὅτι αἱ ἐκκλησίαι εἰσιν οἶκοι ἀγάπης;

   _____

   _____

10. ἐγὼ πέπομφα τοὺς ἀδελφοὺς ἐκ τῶν οἴκων, ἀλλ᾽ οἱ ἄνθρωποι ἐπεποίθεισαν θεὸν αὐτῶν.

    _____

    _____

11. ὑμεῖς ἐγνώκατε ὅτι ὁ θεὸς ὑμῶν ἦν παρ᾽ ὑμῖν.

    _____

    _____

12. οἱ διάκονοι ἀκηκόασιν περὶ τῶν ἁμαρτιῶν τῶν ὄχλων.

    _____

    _____

13. γέγραφά σοι περὶ ἀγάπης, ὑμεῖς δὲ εἴπατέ μοι ὅτι οὐ πεπίστευκα ἐν τῷ κυρίῳ.

    _____

    _____

14. πέπομφα τὰ τέκνα εἰς τὴν ἔρημον ὅτι αὐτὰ ἦσαν κακά.

    _____

    _____

15. ὁ Μεσσίας ἡμῶν εἴρηκεν παραβολὰς καὶ ἀγαθοῖς καὶ ἁμαρτωλοῖς ἐν τῇ συναγωγῇ.

    _____

    _____

16. σέσωκας τοὺς ἀδελφοὺς ἀπὸ τῶν ἁμαρτιῶν αὐτῶν, ἀλλ᾽ εἰρήκει ἀλήθειαν τοῖς τέκνοις.

_____

_____

17. ἀκηκόασιν καὶ οἱ ἄπιστοι καὶ αἱ ἀκάθαρτοι τὴν διδαχὴν τοῦ Χριστοῦ, ἀλλ᾽ αὐτοὶ οὐ πεποίθασιν αὐτόν.

_____

_____

18. ἐγὼ ἑώρακα τὰς ἐπιστολὰς ὅτι ὁ ἀπόστολος ἐγέγραπτο πρὸς τοὺς ἀδελφοὺς ἐν τοῖς οἴκοις αὐτῶν.

_____

_____

19. εὕρηκεν ὁ ἄγγελος τοῦ κυρίου ὑπομονὴν ἐν τῇ διακονίᾳ αὐτῆς.

_____

_____

20. εἰμὶ ὁ ἄνθρωπος ὅτι πέπονθεν τὴν ὀργὴν τῶν πονηρῶν ὄχλων.

_____

_____

21. ὁ θεὸς αὐτὸς σέσωκεν τὸν κόσμον, πέφευγα δὲ παρὰ αὐτοῦ.

_____

_____

22. εἴρηκας τὰς ἐντολὰς τοῦ κυρίου ἡμῶν καὶ τοῖς τέκνοις καὶ τοῖς δούλοις;

_____

_____

23. πεπιστεύκαμεν ἐν τῇ ἀληθείᾳ, καὶ ἡ ἀλήθεια ἐθεράπευσεν ἡμᾶς.

_____

_____

24. αὐτὸς ἐπεποίθει μοι, ἀλλ' ἡμάρτηκα ὅτι εἰμὶ ἄπιστος ἄνθρωπος.

25. οἱ ἀπόστολοι ἐδίδασκον ὅτι ὁ Ἰησοῦς πέπονθεν καὶ ἡτοίμακεν σωτηρίαν ὑπὲρ ἡμῶν.

26. οἱ ἄγγελοι οἱ κακοὶ εἴρηκαν ταῖς γλώσσαις ἀνθρώπου.

27. ᾔδειτε τοὺς νεανίας καὶ ἑωράκατε τὰς δόξας τοῦ κυρίου.

28. οἱ διάκονοι πεπιστεύκεισαν τὰς ἀληθείας περὶ τοῦ υἱοῦ τοῦ θεοῦ, ἀλλ' οὐχ εὕρηκεν ἡ καρδία αὐτοῦ εἰρήνην.

29. οἱ ἅγιοι οἴδασιν τὴν μόνην ὁδὸν τῆς σωτηρίας ὅτι οὐ πεποίθασιν ἐν τοῖς θεοῖς τῆς γῆς.

30. εἴρηκα περὶ τῆς ψυχῆς μου καὶ τοῖς προφήταις καὶ τοῖς ἀγγέλοις.

31. ἐγὼ πιστεύω ὅτι ἀκήκοας τὴν φωνὴν τοῦ θεοῦ, ἀλλὰ σὺ οὐ πιστεύεις αὐτήν.

32. αὐταὶ ἀκηκόασιν ὅτι ἡ κεφαλὴ τῆς ἐκκλησίας ἐστιν ὁ Ἰησοῦς Χριστός, ἀλλ' ἐγὼ οὐκ ἀκήκοα τὴν ἀλήθειαν Χριστοῦ.

_____

_____

33. ὑμεῖς εἰρήκατε ὅτι ὁ νόμος τοῦ ἀνθρώπου σῴζει ψυχάς, ἀλλ' ἐγὼ λέγω ὑμῖν ὅτι ὁ νόμος νεκρός.

_____

_____

34. ἡτοίμακα τὰς συναγωγὰς ὑπὲρ τοῦ Πέτρου, καὶ οἴδασιν τοὺς ὁδοὺς αὐτοῦ.

_____

_____

35. ὁ νεὸς δεδίδαχεν τὰς ἐπιστολὰς τοῖς ἑτέροις μαθηταῖς περὶ τῆς δικαιοσύνης τοῦ θεοῦ;

_____

_____

36. πέφευγα ἐκ τοῦ ἱεροῦ τοῦ θανάτου ὅτι οἱ θεοὶ τοῦ λίθου οὐκ ἦσαν καλοί.

_____

37. σὺ ἔγνωκας πιστὰ καὶ ἐγὼ ἔγνωκα πιστά, ἀλλ' ἐγὼ οὐ ἀκήκοα αὐτὰ ἀπὸ σοῦ.

_____

_____

38. μακάριός ἐστιν ὁ ἄνθρωπος ὅτι ἑώρακεν τὸν κύριον καὶ εἴρηκεν αὐτῷ.

_____

_____

39. ὁ κύριος ἑώρακεν τὰς ζωὰς τῶν ἀκαθάρτων δούλων, εἰρήκασιν δὲ κατὰ αὐτοῦ καὶ οὐκ οἴδασιν τὸν ἅγιον.

_____

_____

40. σὺ πέποιθας τὰς πονηράς, πεποίθαμεν δὲ τοὺς δυνατούς.

_____

_____

ENGLISH to GREEK

Provide the Greek translation for each English sentence.

1. You (sg.) have trusted in the work of the Son of God.

   _____

   _____

2. The peace of the soldiers has sent the children to Christ.

   _____

   _____

3. We have known both the truth of the Lord and the glory of Jesus.

   _____

   _____

4. The disciple has learned about the ways of our covenant.

   _____

   _____

5. You (pl.) were knowing (use a form of οἶδα) that the hypocrites were teaching in the evil temple.

   _____

   _____

6. I have not heard the teaching about the gifts of life.

   _____

   _____

7. The strong woman has not prepared her heart for the kingdom.

_____

_____

8. We have believed the words of the gospel.

_____

_____

9. I have sinned, but He has saved me.

_____

_____

10. They know (use a form of οἶδα) that the crowd has not believed them.

_____

_____

11

DEMONSTRATIVE PRONOUNS

MATCHING

Choose the best answer.

____ 1. near demonstrative pronoun

____ 2. remote demonstrative pronoun

____ 3. arthrous noun

____ 4. anarthrous noun

____ 5. ταῦτα

____ 6. ἐκεῖνα

____ 7. οὗτοι

____ 8. ἐκεῖνοι

____ 9. αὕτη

____10. αὐτή

A. ἄνθρωπος

B. "she"

C. "these (things)"

D. "this" (feminine)

E. ὁ ἄνθρωπος

F. οὗτος

G. ἐκεῖνος

H. "those (things)"

I. "those" (masc)

J. "these" (masc)

MULTIPLE CHOICE

Choose the best answer.

___ 1. The Latin root of "demonstrative" is *demonstro*, which means _____.

    A. "I touch"   B. "I point out"   C. "the demon"   D. "I call out"

___ 2. Which form is a demonstrative pronoun (there may be more than one form)?

    A. αὐτή   B. ταύτας   C. αὐται   D. αὐταί

___ 3. Demonstrative pronouns contain rough breathing marks in the _____ form.

    A. masc. pl. nom.   B. masc. sg. nom. C. fem. sg. & pl. nom.   D. all of the above

___ 4. The declension of ἐκεῖνος is identical to that of _____.

    A. αὐτός   B. ἡμέρα   C. δῶρον   D. none of the above

___ 5. The correct translation for ἐκείναις is _____.

    A. "of these women" B. "to that thing" C. "by those men"   D. "to those women"

___ 6. The correct translation for ταῦτα is _____.

    A. "this thing"   B. "that thing"   C. "these things"   D. "those things"

___ 7. The correct translation for οὗτος ὁ μαθητής is _____.

    A. "that disciple"   B. "this disciple" C. "to that disciple" D. "those disciples"

___ 8. Which form is feminine?

    A. ἐκείνας   B. ἐκεῖνα   C. ταῦτα   D. τούτου

___ 9. The correct translation of αὕτη is _____.

    A. "this woman"   B. "that woman" C. "she"   D. "this thing"

___ 10. The correct translation αὐταί is _____.

    A. "they"   B. "this woman" C. "she"   D. "these women"

TRUE/FALSE

Indicate whether the statement is true or false.

____ 1. Pronouns are used to avoid the repetitious stating of the main verb.

____ 2. There are nine classes of pronouns in the New Testament.

____ 3. The near demonstrative is translated with the word "that."

____ 4. The only difference between feminine nominative demonstrative pronouns and feminine nominative personal pronouns is the presence or absence of an iota subscript.

____ 5. The demonstrative pronoun must agree with its antecedent in gender and number but not case.

____ 6. The demonstrative pronoun always modifies arthrous nouns.

____ 7. The demonstrative pronoun always occurs in the predicate position.

____ 8. The demonstrative pronoun can never be anarthrous.

____ 9. The demonstrative pronoun can sometimes be translated with "he," "she," or "they."

____10. The special use of a demonstrative pronoun allows a demonstrative occasionally to be translated as "same" or a form of "self."

GREEK to ENGLISH

Provide the English translation for each Greek sentence.

1. ἡ βασιλεία τοῦ οὐρανοῦ οὐκ ἔστιν τόπος ἐν τούτῳ τῷ κόσμῳ, ἀλλ᾽ ὁ αὐτὸς Μεσσίας ἐθεράπευεν τοὺς λαοὺς ταύτης τῆς βασιλείας ἀπὸ τῶν ἁμαρτιῶν αὐτῶν.

    _____

    _____

2. οὐκ ἐπιστεύσαμεν ὅτι θεὸς ἡτοίμασεν ἐκείνην τὴν ὁδὸν ὑπὲρ ἡμῶν.

    _____

    _____

3. Ἰησοῦς Χριστὸς ἔβαλεν τὸν ἐχθρὸν ἐκ οὐρανοῦ, ἀλλ᾽ οὗτος διδάσκει τὸν λαὸν αὐτοῦ κατὰ τὴν ἀλήθειαν.

    _____

    _____

4. ἐκεῖνοι οἱ δοῦλοι ἐδόξασαν τὸν θεὸν ἐν τῷ ναῷ μετὰ τῶν ἀδελφῶν αὐτῶν;

    _____

    _____

5. αὕτη οὐ γράψει βιβλίον, αὐτὴ δὲ ἐθεράπευεν τὰς καρδίας τῶν αὐτῶν τυφλῶν.

    _____

    _____

6. οὗτος ὁ Χριστός ἐστιν ὁ ἀμνὸς τοῦ θεοῦ καὶ σώσει τὰ τέκνα αὐτοῦ ἀπὸ θανάτου.

    _____

    _____

7. ἐκείνη ἡ ἐκκλησία κηρύσσει τοὺς λόγους τῶν γραφῶν καὶ πέμπει ἐκείνας εἰς τὸν κόσμον.

    _____

    _____

8. τοῦτο τὸ δαιμόνιον, ἐκεῖνο τὸ δαιμόνιον, τὰ δαιμόνια ταῦτα, καὶ τὰ δαιμόνια ἐκεῖνα γινώσκουσιν τὰς ἀληθείας ἐν τῷ βιβλίῳ τῆς ζωῆς, ἀλλ' αἱ καρδίαι αὐτῶν οὐ πιστεύουσιν ἐν αὐταῖς.

    _____

    _____

9. οὗτοι οἱ θεοὶ τοῦ λίθου ἄξουσιν τοὺς λαοὺς εἰς ζωὴν ἁμαρτίας καὶ θανάτου, ἐκείνη δὲ ἔχει ἑτέραν εἰρήνην ἐν τῇ καρδίᾳ αὐτῆς.

    _____

    _____

10. τὰ δαιμόνια πεφεύγασιν ἐκ τῶν τόπων τῶν ἁγίων καὶ εἰς τὴν ἔρημον.

    _____

    _____

11. ὁ φίλος τῶν μαθητῶν πέπονθεν διὰ τὰς ἁμαρτίας τῶν πονηρῶν ἀνθρώπων, αὗται δὲ εὗρον τὴν σωτηρίαν τοῦ κυρίου ἡμῶν.

    _____

    _____

12. ὁ δίκαιος τυφλὸς ἔγραψεν ταῦτα τὰ σημεῖα τοῖς παιδίοις περὶ τῆς ἀγάπης τοῦ Χριστοῦ.

    _____

    _____

13. ὁ κύριος τοῦ σαββάτου ἐστὶν ὁ αὐτὸς κύριος τοῦ σταυροῦ καὶ τῆς βασιλείας τοῦ οὐρανοῦ;

    _____

    _____

14. ταῦτα τὰ πλοῖα ἄξουσιν τοὺς στρατιώτας εἰς τὴν θάλασσαν, ἀλλ' ἐκεῖνοι οἱ ἐχθροὶ οὐ βλέπουσιν ταῦτα τὰ πλοῖα διὰ τὸν ἥλιον ἐν τοῖς οὐρανοῖς.

    _____

    _____

15. ἐκεῖναι ἔγραψαν τὰ μυστήρια ἐν τοῖς βιβλίοις, ἀλλ' ἐκεῖνα οὐκ ἐδίδαξεν τοὺς υἱοὺς αὐτῶν περὶ τῶν ἐντολῶν τοῦ θεοῦ.

_____

_____

16. ἐκεῖνος ὁ ἄνθρωπός ἐστιν ὁ καλὸς Μεσσίας, ἀλλ' ἡ βασιλεία αὐτοῦ οὐκ ἔστιν ἐκ ταύτης τῆς γῆς.

_____

_____

17. ὁ θρόνος τούτου τοῦ θεοῦ ἐστιν ὑπὲρ τὰς ὁδοὺς τούτου τοῦ διαβόλου, καὶ οἱ ὀφθαλμοὶ τοῦ ἁγίου εἰσὶν ἐπὶ ἕκαστον ἄνθρωπον.

_____

_____

18. ὁ αὐτὸς ἥλιος ἑτοιμάσει τὴν γῆν ὑπὲρ καρπῶν καὶ φέρει ζωὴν τῷ λαῷ ἐκείνης τῆς γῆς.

_____

_____

19. οἱ στρατιῶται ἐξέβαλλον τὸν τυφλὸν ἐκ τοῦ ἱεροῦ μετὰ τοῦ ἱματίου αὐτοῦ ὅτι οἱ στρατιῶται ἐκείνου τοῦ ἱεροῦ οὐκ ἔχουσιν ἔργον ὑπὲρ τοῦ ἀνθρώπου.

_____

_____

20. οὗτοί εἰσιν οἱ λαοὶ ἀληθείας καὶ ἀγάπης καὶ εἰρήνης, ἀλλ' ἐκεῖναί εἰσιν οἱ ἐχθροὶ τοῦ θεοῦ τοῦ σαββάτου.

_____

_____

21. ὁ Πέτρος εἶπεν τοὺς λόγους τοὺς δυνατοὺς καὶ τοῖς τυφλοῖς τῆς γῆς καὶ τοῖς παιδίοις τοῦ σταυροῦ;

_____

_____

22. εὕρηκας ἐκείνους τοὺς ἀγρούς, ἡτοίμακα δὲ αὐτοὺς ὑπὲρ τοῦ κυρίου καὶ τῶν μαθητῶν αὐτοῦ.

_____

_____

23. οὗτος ὁ διάβολός ἐστιν ὁ ἐχθρὸς ἡμῶν, ἀλλ᾽ ὁ θεὸς τῆς ἀληθείας σώσει τὰς ψυχὰς τῶν λαῶν αὐτοῦ ἐν ἐκείναις ταῖς ἡμέραις.

_____

_____

24. ὁ Ἰησοῦς οἶδεν τὸν χρόνον τῆς βασιλείας, γινώσκω δὲ τὰ σημεῖα τῶν καιρῶν.

_____

_____

25. ἐκεῖνος ὁ προφήτης οὐκ ἐδόξασεν τὰς ἀληθείας περὶ τοῦ μόνου θεοῦ, καὶ τὰ τέκνα τὰ πονηρὰ οὐκ ἐδίδαξεν περὶ τῆς σωτηρίας τοῦ Χριστοῦ.

_____

_____

26. αὕτη ἡ προσευχὴ ἄξει τὸν ἁμαρτωλὸν πρὸς σωτηρίαν κατὰ τὰς γραφάς.

_____

_____

27. οἱ φόβοι ἐκείνων τῶν παιδίων φεύγουσιν παρὰ αὐτῶν ὅτι ταῦτα ἤκουσαν τὴν φωνὴν τοῦ δυνατοῦ φίλου αὐτῶν.

_____

_____

28. τοῦτο τὸ δῶρόν ἐστιν δῶρον εἰρήνης καὶ ζωῆς ὑπὲρ σοῦ καὶ ἐμοῦ.

_____

_____

29. ἐσθίουσιν καὶ καρποὺς καὶ ἄρτους ἐν τῷ οἴκῳ τῶν ἁμαρτωλῶν;

_____

_____

30. ὁ νεανίας ἐκεῖνος ἀπέθανεν, καὶ ἠνέγκαμεν ἀγαθὰ δῶρα τοῖς φίλοις ἐκείνου τοῦ ἀνθρώπου.

_____

_____

31. ἐκηρύξαμεν ἐν ταῖς ἡμέραις τοῦ Ἰησοῦ περὶ τοῦ ἁγίου υἱοῦ τοῦ θεοῦ, ἀλλ' ὁ Πέτρος εἶπεν λόγους θανάτου ἀντὶ τούτων τῶν λόγων τῆς ἀληθείας.

_____

_____

32. ὁ βιβλίον τῆς ἀληθείας λέγει περὶ τοῦ ἀμνοῦ τοῦ θεοῦ καὶ ἤγαγεν τοὺς υἱοὺς τοῦ θεοῦ καὶ τοὺς υἱοὺς τῶν ἀνθρώπων εἰς τὸν τόπον ἐκείνης τῆς εἰρήνης.

_____

_____

33. ἐγὼ εἶδον τὸν ἥλιον ἐν τοῖς οὐρανοῖς, καὶ αὕτη εἶπον ὅτι ἐκεῖνος ὁ θεός ἐστιν ὑπὲρ τοὺς οὐρανοὺς καὶ τὴν γῆν.

_____

_____

34. τὸ ἱμάτιον ἔλιπεν τὴν κεφαλὴν τοῦ προφήτου καὶ ἐθεράπευσεν τοῦτο τὸ παιδίον ἐκείνου τοῦ δούλου.

_____

_____

35. τοῦτο τὸ εὐαγγέλιον δοξάζει τὸν κύριον καὶ λύσει ἐκεῖνον τὸν λαὸν παρὰ τοῦ νόμου τοῦ θανάτου κατὰ τὰς γραφάς.

_____

_____

36. οἱ διάκονοι τῆς συναγωγῆς ἐκείνης οὐ ἔμαθον τὰς ἀληθείας τῶν γραφῶν τούτων.

_____

_____

37. ἐκεῖνος ὁ προφήτης ἐστὶν ἁμαρτωλός, καὶ ἐκεῖνοι οἱ μαθηταί εἰσι κακοί.

_____

_____

38. σὺ εἶ ἄνθρωπος μετὰ τὴν καρδίαν τοῦ θεοῦ, καὶ οἱ καρποὶ τοῦ ἔργου σου δοξάσουσιν τὸν θρόνον τοῦ θεοῦ.

_____

_____

39. οὗτος ὁ ἄρτος ἐστὶν ἡ καινὴ διαθήκη ὅτι ἀπέθανεν ὑπὲρ σοῦ.

_____

_____

40. αὗται ἡτοιμάκασι τὴν ὁδὸν τοῦ κυρίου ὑπὲρ τῶν ὄχλων, ἀλλ᾽ ἐκεῖναι ἔλαβον ταῦτα τὰ δῶρα ἀπὸ ἐκείνων τῶν ἀνθρώπων.

_____

_____

ENGLISH to GREEK

Provide the Greek translation for each English sentence.

1. Are these the same commandments of the Lord?

_____

_____

2. This evil man does not glorify the Lord of heaven and earth.

_____

_____

3. The holy apostle opens the eyes of these blind men and heals their sins.

_____

_____

4. The devil and his demons proclaim that this way of sin and that way of truth are the same way.

_____

_____

5. The hearts of those people received love and joy from this Son of God.

_____

_____

6. We prepare the way for those men according to those Scriptures.

_____

_____

7. I said these things to you (sg.), but you (pl.) did not believe in them.

_____

_____

8. You heard these words, but did you see those signs from heaven with your eyes?

_____

_____

9. My head heard those truths of Christ, and my heart has trusted in the God of these Scriptures.

_____

_____

10. My eyes have seen the same glory of the Lord, but my friend has not believed in the same truth.

_____

_____

Present Middle and Passive Indicative

MATCHING

Choose the best answer.

___	1. passive voice	A.	"I am loosing"
___	2. middle voice	B.	two parties are necessary for action (e.g., δέχομαι, "I welcome")
___	3. active voice	C.	expressed by ὑπό and the genitive
___	4. deponent verb	D.	describes a process that the subject alone can experience (e.g., βούλομαι, "I wish")
___	5. deponent of reciprocity	E.	"I am being loosed"
___	6. deponent of reflexivity	F.	expressed by the dative case
___	7. deponent of self-involvement	G.	expressed by διά and the genitive
___	8. direct agent	H.	a verb that is middle/passive in form but active in meaning
___	9. intermediate agent	I.	the verbal idea turns back upon the subject (e.g., τυφόομαι, "I am conceited")
___	10. impersonal agent	J.	"I myself am loosing"

MULTIPLE CHOICE

Choose the best answer.

____ 1. The phrase "I am loosing" is translated in which voice?

     A. active   B. middle   C. subjunctive   D. passive

____ 2. Which of the following is not a recognized voice in the Greek language?

     A. active   B. middle   C. subjunctive   D. passive

____ 3. Which of the following is NOT a primary middle suffix?

     A. τε   B. μεθα   C. νται   D. σθε

____ 4. The stem λυ + connecting vowel ε + and primary middle suffix σαι come together to make the final form _____.

     A. λυέσθω   B. λύῃ   C. λῦσαι   D. λυέσαι

____ 5. An accurate translation of λύομαι is _____.

     A. "I have loosed"   B. "I have been loosed"   C. "I am being loosed"   D. "I was loosing"

____ 6. The translation of a reflexive middle verb is _____.

     A. "I am being loosed"   B. "I myself loose"   C. "I loose for myself"   D. "I loose myself"

____ 7. The translation of an intensive middle verb is _____.

     A. "I am being loosed"   B. "I myself loose"   C. "I loose for myself"   D. "I loose myself"

____ 8. The translation of a reciprocal middle verb is _____.

     A. "they are being loosed"   B. "they themselves loose"   C. "they loose for themselves"   D. "they loose one another"

____ 9. The correct translation of the Greek word βούλομαι is _____.

     A. "I am being wished"   B. "I wish for myself"   C. "I myself wish"   D. "I wish"

____ 10. The phrase "I am being healed" is translated in which voice?

     A. active   B. middle   C. subjunctive   D. passive

TRUE/FALSE

Indicate whether the statement is true or false.

___ 1. The middle and passive forms of present tense indicative verbs are identical.

___ 2. All middle and passive indicative forms take the negative μή instead of οὐ.

___ 3. Verbs that are deponent in the present tense cannot be deponent in other tenses.

___ 4. When parsing a present deponent verb, the mood should be noted as "deponent."

___ 5. Many of the deponent verbs occur with an *adjectival* prefix.

___ 6. Deponent verbs sometimes take a direct object in a case other than accusative.

___ 7. If the words ὑπό, διά, or ἐν are not located in a sentence, the verb cannot be translated passively.

___ 8. The deponent verb γίνομαι takes a complement.

___ 9. An intensive middle translation in Greek can be expressed by both a middle voice verb and an intensive use of αὐτός.

___10. ἔρχομαι can be translated "I myself am coming" or "I am being overcome."

GREEK to ENGLISH

Provide the English translation for each Greek sentence.

1. ἡ ψυχή μου σώζεται ὑπὸ τοῦ ἀγαθοῦ κυρίου, ἀλλ' ἡ καρδία σου ἑτοιμάζεται τῷ λόγῳ τῆς ἀληθείας.

   _____

   _____

2. ὁ διάβολος ὁ πονηρὸς ψεύδεται περὶ τῆς ἀληθείας τοῦ εὐαγγελίου, ἀλλὰ γίνομαι ἰσχυρὸν μαρτυρίον πρὸς τοὺς φίλους ἐμοῦ.

   _____

   _____

3. τὰ παιδία ἐξέρχονται ἐκ τῶν ἱερῶν ὅτι ἐκβάλλονται ὑπὸ τῶν ἐχθρῶν τοῦ κυρίου.

   _____

   _____

4. ὁ τυφλὸς θεραπεύεται τὸ τέκνον τῶν προφητῶν, ἀλλ' αὐτὸς οὐ θεραπεύεται διὰ τῶν προφητῶν.

   _____

   _____

5. ἀσπάζεται ἄνθρωπον θεοῦ, καὶ ἔρχῃ ἀγαθῷ μαθητῇ ὅτι προσεύχεται προσευχὴν τῷ θεῷ ἐν ἑτέρᾳ γλώσσῃ.

   _____

   _____

6. ἡμεῖς ψευδόμεθα τοῖς μαθηταῖς τοῖς ἁγίοις καὶ τοῖς προφήταις, ἐγὼ δὲ διδάσκω τοὺς νεανίας περὶ τὴν θάλασσαν.

   _____

   _____

7. ψεύδεσθε ὅτι λέγετε ὅτι ἡ πιστὴ οὐ διδάσκει τὴν ἀλήθειαν διὰ τούτων τῶν μαθητῶν.

   _____

   _____

8. ἡ ἄξια διδαχὴ τοῦ προφήτου γράφεται ὑπὸ τῶν νεανιῶν, ἀλλ' οὐ πιστεύεται τὰς ἀληθείας.

   _____

   _____

9. ὁ κύριος αὐτὸς διδάσκει τὰ τέκνα αὐτοῦ, καὶ ὁ κύριος ἑτοιμάζεται τὰ τέκνα ὑπὲρ θανάτου.

   _____

   _____

10. Ἰησοῦς Χριστὸς κηρύσσεται καὶ οἱ μαθηταὶ φέρονται τοὺς λόγους τοῖς στρατιώταις ἐν τῇ ἐρήμῳ.

    _____

    _____

11. καθ' ἡμέραν ἡ ἐκκλησία προσεύχεται ἐν ταῖς συναγωγαῖς καὶ ἐν τῷ ναῷ ὑπὲρ τῶν ψυχῶν τῶν τέκνων αὐτῶν.

    _____

    _____

12. τὰ μυστήρια τῶν ἀνθρώπων εὑρίσκονται τοῖς ὀφθαλμοῖς τοῦ δυνατοῦ θεοῦ.

    _____

    _____

13. αἱ ἄπιστοι ἀσπάζονται τοὺς κυρίους αὐτῶν σὺν χαρᾷ, ἀλλ' οἱ κύριοι αὐτῶν οὐ λαμβάνουσιν τὴν μαρτυρίαν αὐτῶν ὅτι αὗται ἔρχονται σὺν ἀκαθάρτοις καρδίαις.

    _____

    _____

14. οὗτος ὁ στρατιώτης εὑρίσκεται διὰ τῶν κυρίων αὐτοῦ ἐν τῇ ἐρήμῳ ὅτι ὁ κύριος αὐτοῦ βούλεται πονηρὰ ἐπὶ αὐτοῖς.

    _____

    _____

15. δέχεσθε τοὺς νεοὺς λόγους ἀπὸ τοῦ βιβλίου τῆς ζωῆς ἀντὶ τῆς διδαχῆς τῆς πονηρᾶς.

_____

_____

16. ἄγεται ὑπὸ τῶν ἐχθρῶν αὐτοῦ εἰς τὴν ἔρημον, καὶ οἱ ἐχθροὶ αὐτοῦ φέρουσιν ὀργὴν ἐπὶ αὐτῷ.

_____

_____

17. ὁ Μεσσίας εὐαγγελίζεται καὶ τοῖς ἀνθρώποις καὶ τοῖς δαιμονίοις, ἀλλ' ὁ ἄνθρωπος ὁ ἀγαθὸς πιστεύεται τὰς ἀληθείας τοῦ θεοῦ.

_____

_____

18. αἱ ἐπιστολαὶ ἀνοίγονται ὑπὸ τοῦ Πέτρου, καὶ αὐτὸς ἑτοιμάζεται τὰς καρδίας τῶν μαθητῶν ὑπὲρ τῆς διακονίας.

_____

_____

19. ὁ δοῦλος ἐργάζεται ἐν τῷ ἀγρῷ ὅτι οὐχ ἕξει φόβον ἐν ταῖς ἐσχάταις ἡμέραις.

_____

_____

20. τὰ σημεῖα τῶν χρόνων γράφεται ὑπὸ τοῦ σοφοῦ προφήτου ἐν τῷ βιβλίῳ τῆς ζωῆς.

_____

_____

21. ὑμεῖς ἐκπορεύεσθε ἐκ τῶν οἴκων ὑμῶν, ἀλλ' ἐξέρχονται ἐκ τοῦ οἴκου ἐμοῦ.

_____

_____

22. πορεύεσθε πρὸς τὸν θρόνον τοῦ θεοῦ, ἡ δὲ ἀλήθεια οὐκ ἀκούεται ὅτι οἱ πονηροὶ μαθηταὶ ψεύδονται τοῖς λαοῖς περὶ τῆς ὁδοῦ τῆς σωτηρίας.

_____

_____

23. ὁ ἀγαπητὸς υἱὸς ἀποκρίνεται τοῖς σοφοῖς ἀνθρώποις, οὐ δὲ πείσει τὸν Χριστόν.

_____

_____

24. ὁ ἀμνὸς τοῦ θεοῦ δοξάζεται ἐπὶ τῇ γῇ ὅτι σώζεται ἁμαρτωλοὺς ἀπὸ τῶν ἁμαρτιῶν αὐτῶν.

_____

_____

25. οἱ ἀπόστολοι εὐαγγελίζονται ἐν τῷ κόσμῳ καὶ θεὸς σώζεται τοὺς υἱοὺς τῆς γῆς.

_____

_____

26. βαπτίζομαι ὑπὸ τοῦ ἀποστόλου ἐν τῇ θαλάσσῃ, καὶ ὁ **Φίλιππος** κηρύσσεται τὸ εὐαγγέλιον τοῖς τυφλοῖς ἐν τῷ ἱερῷ.

_____

_____

27. τὰ τέκνα προσεύχεται ὑπὲρ τῆς σωτηρίας τῶν φίλων αὐτῶν ἀλλ' ἐκβάλλεται ἐκ τῶν ἱερῶν.

_____

_____

28. ἐκεῖνα τὰ τέκνα ἐστὶν ὑποκριταὶ ὅτι προσεύχονται ὑπὲρ τῆς σωτηρίας τῶν φίλων αὐτῶν, ἀλλ' αὐτὰ ἔλιπον τὴν πρώτην ἀγάπην αὐτῶν.

_____

_____

29. οὐ ψεύδομαι περὶ ἐκείνων τῶν τέκνων, ἀλλ᾽ ὁ θεὸς ἐθεράπευσέν με ἀπὸ τῆς ὀργῆς μου.

_____

_____

30. τὰ δαιμόνια ἐξέρχονται ἀπὸ τῶν συναγωγῶν διὰ τὴν δικαίαν μαρτυρίαν τοῦ ἁγίου υἱοῦ τοῦ θεοῦ.

_____

_____

31. αἱ προσευχαὶ τοῦ λαοῦ δοξάσουσι τὸν κύριον, ἀλλ᾽ οὐ προσευχόμεθα μετὰ παρρησίας καὶ χαρᾶς.

_____

_____

32. δέχονται καὶ οἱ κύριοι καὶ οἱ δοῦλοι τὰς ἀληθείας τοῦ θεοῦ ἐν τῷ νόμῳ τοῦ θεοῦ, ἀλλὰ γίνομαι πονηρὸς ἄνθρωπος.

_____

_____

33. ἀσπάζομαι τὴν ἡμέραν μετὰ ἰσχυρᾶς καρδίας καὶ πείσω τὰς ἀληθείας περὶ τοῦ σταυροῦ τοῦ Χριστοῦ.

_____

_____

34. σῴζεται εἰς τὴν βασιλείαν ὑπὸ τοῦ κυρίου, οὐ δὲ πείθομαι τὸ εὐαγγέλιον Ἰησοῦ Χριστοῦ.

_____

_____

35. γίνεσθε ἄνθρωποι θεοῦ καὶ ἄγεσθε τοὺς υἱοὺς τῆς γῆς πρὸς τὸν σταυρὸν Χριστοῦ.

_____

_____

36. ὁ πονηρὸς δοξάζεται, ἀλλ' ὁ υἱὸς τοῦ θεοῦ δοξάζεται ὑπὸ τοῦ δικαίου ἀνθρώπου.

   _____

   _____

37. τὰ τέκνα ἐργάζεται ἐν τοῖς ἀγροῖς ὑπὲρ τῶν φίλων αὐτῶν, ἀλλ' οἱ φίλοι αὐτῶν οὐ βούλονται ἀγαθὰ ἐπὶ αὐτοῖς.

   _____

   _____

38. τὰ βιβλία κηρύσσονται ὑπὸ τῶν ἀποστόλων καὶ τῶν προφητῶν, ἀλλ' αὐτοὶ οὐ γίνονται δίκαιοι διὰ τὴν ἁμαρτίαν ἐν ταῖς καρδίαις αὐτῶν.

   _____

   _____

39. λογίζομαι ἑτέρας ὁδοὺς σωτηρίας, ἀλλ' Ἰησοῦς εἶπεν ὅτι αὐτὸς ἦν ἡ μόνη ὁδὸς οὐρανῷ.

   _____

   _____

40. ἐξέρχεσθε ἐκ τοῦ οἴκου, καὶ εἰσερχόμεθα εἰς τὸν οἶκον ὅτι οἱ ὀφθαλμοί ἡμῶν εἶδον τὸν ἥλιον ἐν τοῖς οὐρανοῖς.

   _____

   _____

ENGLISH to GREEK

Provide the Greek translation for each English sentence.

1. Jesus Christ is being glorified in the hearts and lives of His people.

   _____

   _____

2. I am preaching the commandments of God, but you (sg.) are being taught the ways of truth by your brother.

   _____

   _____

3. I greet the brothers in the Lord, but I do not answer them because they are wishing bad things upon me.

_____

_____

4. The secrets of the heart are being known each day.

_____

_____

5. The blind men come into the temple, but they are not receiving Christ into their hearts.

_____

_____

6. The sinners are being taught about the love of God, and I myself am glorifying God.

_____

_____

7. The children wish for gifts from the men of the church because they themselves are not praying for them.

_____

_____

8. The good news is being preached by messengers, but the good woman is not learning the truths of Christ for herself.

_____

_____

9. You (sg.) are becoming a man of God, and she is a beloved woman.

_____

_____

10. I myself believe in the Son of God, but you (sg.) yourself do not trust in Him.

_____

_____

13

PERFECT MIDDLE AND PASSIVE, FUTURE MIDDLE INDICATIVE

MATCHING

Choose the best answer.

___ 1. πείθομαι

___ 2. πέπεισμαι

___ 3. γνώσομαι

___ 4. ἀκούσεσθε

___ 5. γέγραπται

___ 6. ἄγεσθε

___ 7. ἔσονται

___ 8. ἐρχόμεθα

___ 9. βαπτίζονται

___ 10. πεπόρευσαι

A. Perfect Passive Indicative, 1st person Singular

B. Perfect Passive Indicative, 3rd person Singular

C. Present Deponent Indicative, 1st person Plural

D. Present Passive Indicative, 1st person Singular

E. Future Middle Indicative, 3rd person Plural

F. Perfect Middle Indicative, 2nd person Singular

G. Future Middle Indicative, 2nd person Plural

H. Present Passive Indicative, 3rd person Plural

I. Future Middle Indicative, 1st person Singular

J. Present Passive Indicative, 2nd person Plural

MULTIPLE CHOICE

Choose the best answer.

____ 1. The Greek verb system is comprised of _____ principal parts.

    A. three   B. six   C. twelve   D. twenty-four

____ 2. The perfect middle and passive incorporates the _____ principal part.

    A. second   B. fourth   C. fifth   D. tenth

____ 3. The perfective aspect morpheme in Greek is _____.

    A. amalgamation   B. elision   C. σ   D. κα

____ 4. The translation of πέπεισμαι is _____.

    A. "I have trusted in myself"   B. "I have been trusted in"   C. "I myself have trusted in"   D. all of the above

____ 5. What is the perfect middle/passive indicative, third person singular form of γράφω?

    A. γέγραπται   B. γεγράπεται   C. γεγράφεται   D. γέγραφται

____ 6. The sign of the future tense in Greek is _____.

    A. ε   B. σ   C. κα   D. reduplication

____ 7. The translation of πορεύσομαι is _____.

    A. "I will be gone"   B. "I myself will go"   C. "I will go"   D. both b and c

____ 8. The future indicative of εἰμί is formed on the stem _____.

    A. ειμ   B. ει   C. εσ   D. εισ

____ 9. Which of the following forms can be translated "he will be"?

    A. ἔσεται   B. ἔση   C. εἴσται   D. ἔσται

____ 10. The translation of ἔσομαι is _____.

    A. "I will be"   B. "I myself will"   C. "I will have been"   D. "I will be myself"

TRUE/FALSE

Indicate whether the statement is true or false.

___ 1. The conjunctions μέν and δέ are often used to express *agreement*.

___ 2. The double καί construction cannot be used with middle and passive verbs.

___ 3. A postpositive word (e.g., γάρ) cannot occur first in a Greek sentence or clause.

___ 4. Most adverbs are declinable in form and thus will have twenty-four forms.

___ 5. The first perfect tense forms in Greek contain reduplication, but second perfect tense forms do not require reduplication.

___ 6. Reduplication occurs only in the passive voice forms of the perfect tense.

___ 7. The future tense does not share middle and passive forms.

___ 8. All future tense forms of εἰμί contain a connecting vowel in between the stem and ending.

___ 9. Rules of amalgamation may apply when forming a future middle indicative verb form in Greek.

___10. εἰμί has only present, imperfect, and future forms in the indicative mood in the Greek New Testament.

GREEK to ENGLISH

Provide the English translation for each Greek sentence.

1. ἐσόμεθα ἐν τῷ οἴκῳ τοῦ κυρίου παρὰ τοῖς φίλοις ἡμῶν, ἀλλ᾽ γνώσεσθε τὸν δοῦλον παρὰ τὴν θάλασσαν.

   _____

   _____

2. σήμερον ἀκούσῃ τὰ παιδία, καὶ σὺ διδάξεις τοὺς λόγους τῶν γραφῶν περὶ τῆς διαθήκης τοῦ θεοῦ αὐτοῖς.

   _____

   _____

3. λήμψεσθε τοὺς λαοὺς ἀπὸ τῶν οἴκων αὐτῶν, πεπείσμεθα δὲ ἐν Ἰησοῦ Χριστῷ ὑπὲρ τῶν ἁμαρτιῶν ἡμῶν.

   _____

   _____

4. γέγραπται μὲν ὁ προφήτης ταύτην τὴν ἀλήθειαν, ὁ δὲ μαθητὴς αὐτοῦ μεμάθηκεν τὸ εὐαγγέλιον ἀπὸ τῆς ἀρχῆς.

   _____

   _____

5. γέγραπται Φίλιππος ἐπιστολὰς περὶ τῆς διδαχῆς τοῦ Πέτρου, ἀλλ᾽ οἱ ὄχλοι οὐκ πιστεύουσιν αὐτὴν ὅτι γνώσονται τὰς ἐπιστολὰς τοῦ Πέτρου ἐν τῷ βιβλίῳ.

   _____

   _____

6. αὐτὸς εἶπεν ὅτι ἐγὼ οὐχί εἰμι θεός, βαπτίζω δὲ κατὰ τὴν ἐντολὴν τοῦ κυρίου.

   _____

   _____

7. οἱ ὀφθαλμοὶ ἐμοῦ βλέψονται τὴν δόξαν τοῦ θεοῦ καθὼς αὐτὸς εἶπεν.

   _____

   _____

8. ἔγνωσται τὰ μυστήρια τῶν σοφῶν ἀνθρώπων ὑπὸ τῶν διακονῶν ἐν ταῖς συναγωγαῖς αὐτῶν.

_____

_____

9. κηρύξεις τὸ εὐαγγέλιον σὺν τοῖς ἔργοις ὑμῶν καθὼς ὁ νόμος εἶπεν, ἀλλ᾽ οὐ λέλυσαι παρὰ τῶν ἔργων τοῦ νόμου.

_____

_____

10. φάγονται οὖν τοὺς λίθους τοῦ ἀνθρώπου ὅτι γέγραπται ἐν τοῖς βιβλίοις τοῦ νόμου.

_____

_____

11. ὁ ἁμαρτωλὸς οὐχ ἡτοίμακεν καλῶς ὅτι οὐκ ἀκήκοεν οὐδὲ πείσεται τὸν λόγον τοῦ κυρίου.

_____

_____

12. τὰ δαιμόνια καὶ ἐκεῖνοι οἱ ἐχθροὶ τοῦ θεοῦ εὑρίσκονται ἐν τῷ οὐρανῷ καὶ φεύγουσιν ὑπὲρ τῶν ζώων αὐτῶν.

_____

_____

13. σὺ οὐκέτι ἔσῃ ὁ ἐχθρὸς τοῦ θεοῦ, καὶ νῦν οἱ ἀδελφοί σου ἔσονται οἱ φίλοι τοῦ κυρίου.

_____

_____

14. ὁ θάνατος τοῦ Χριστοῦ ἐπὶ τοῦ σταυροῦ εἴρηται δι᾽ ἑκάστου τέκνου θεοῦ, καὶ Πέτρος αὐτὸς γράψει περὶ τοῦ θανάτου αὐτοῦ τοῖς ἀνθρώποις τῆς γῆς.

_____

_____

15. νῦν γινώσκω τὴν εἰρήνην τοῦ θεοῦ ἐν τῇ ζωῇ μου, οὐ δὲ ἔγνωσται νεκρὸς ταύτην τὴν ἀλήθειαν παρὰ τῆς ἀρχῆς.

_____

_____

16. ἔγνωσται ἡ μαρτυρία τῶν ἀποστόλων ὑπὸ τῷ ὄχλῳ τῷ ἀγαπητῷ, ἀλλ᾽ οὐ γνωσόμεθα τὰ μυστήρια τοῦ θεοῦ.

_____

_____

17. γνωσόμεθα ἑκάστην ἁμαρτίαν ὅτι οὐκ ἄξουσιν ἡμᾶς εἰς τὴν σωτηρίαν τοῦ κυρίου.

_____

_____

18. ἦτε ὑποκριταὶ ἀλλὰ λέλυσαι ὑπὸ Χριστοῦ;

_____

_____

19. δῶρα καρποῦ καὶ ἄρτου ἀπὸ τοῦ ἀγροῦ βέβληται διὰ τῶν υἱῶν τῶν ἀγαθῶν τοῖς τέκνοις τοῖς μικροῖς ὅτι ἐκεῖνα τὰ τέκνα ἔχει ἀγάπην ὑπὲρ θεοῦ ἐν ταῖς καρδίαις αὐτῶν.

_____

_____

20. ἡτοίμασται τὸ παιδίον ὑπὲρ τῆς διακονίας, διὸ ἐγὼ ἔσομαι ἄνθρωπος θεοῦ καὶ ἀκούσομαι φωνὴν θεοῦ.

_____

_____

21. καθὼς ὁ στρατιώτης ἐκήρυξεν τὴν ἀλήθειαν τοῖς ἁμαρτωλοῖς ἐπὶ τῆς ὁδοῦ, πεπίστευμαι τὰς ἀληθείας Χριστοῦ.

_____

_____

22. οἱ τυφλοὶ λήμψονται τοὺς φίλους παρὰ τῆς ἐρήμου, ἀλλ᾽ οἱ ἕτεροι βλέψονται τὸν θεὸν σὺν τοῖς ὀφθαλμοῖς αὐτῶν.

_____

_____

23. τὰ μυστήρια τῆς ἀρχῆς τῆς ἐντολῆς εὕρηται ἐν τοῖς βιβλίοις ἀλλὰ βέβληται ἐκ τῶν συναγωγῶν ὅτι εὕρηται αὐτά.

_____

_____

24. δοξάσομεν τὸν κύριον ἐν οὐρανῷ, καὶ ἀποθανεῖται ὑπὲρ τῆς γῆς.

_____

_____

25. ἕξουσιν οὐδὲ ζωὴν οὐδὲ εἰρήνην διὰ τὰς ἁμαρτίας αὐτῶν καὶ τὰς ἐπιθυμίας τὰς πονηρὰς αὐτῶν.

_____

_____

26. ἡ διακονία τῶν ἀγγέλων ἤκουσται ὑπὸ τῶν λαῶν ἀντὶ τῆς διδαχῆς τοῦ Ἰησοῦ.

_____

_____

27. ὁ ἄνθρωπος ἐβαπτίζοντο τὰ παιδία παρὰ τὴν θάλασσαν κατὰ τὸν λόγον καὶ τὴν ἐντολὴν τοῦ θεοῦ.

_____

_____

28. σέσωται ὁ δοῦλος ἐκεῖνος ὑπὸ τοῦ Χριστοῦ, οὐ δὲ δοξάσουσιν τὸν θεὸν αὐτῶν ἐν οὐρανῷ.

_____

_____

29. βλέψονται τὴν βασιλείαν τοῦ οὐρανοῦ, καὶ αὐτή ἐστιν τόπος δικαιοσύνης καὶ χαρᾶς.

    _____

    _____

30. λέγουσιν οἱ καρποὶ τῆς δικαιοσύνης σὺν ἰσχυρᾷ φωνῇ, τὰ δὲ ἔργα τῆς ὀργῆς ἡτοίμασται ὑπὸ τοῦ διαβόλου.

    _____

    _____

31. ἐν τῇ ἡμέρᾳ τοῦ κυρίου οἱ ὄχλοι περὶ τὸν θρόνον ἔσονται ἡ ἐκκλησία καὶ γνώσονται τὴν δόξαν τοῦ θεοῦ.

    _____

    _____

32. αὕτη ἡ σωτηρία ἔγνωσται ὑφ᾽ ἑκάστου ἀνθρώπου ἐπὶ τῆς γῆς.

    _____

    _____

33. ἡ ἀλήθεια γέγραπται ἐπὶ τῶν καρδιῶν τῶν λαῶν τῆς ἐκκλησίας καθὼς αὐτὸς εἶπεν παρὰ τῆς ἀρχῆς.

    _____

    _____

34. σήμερον ὁ Ἰησοῦς λήμψεται τὴν ψυχὴν τοῦ μικροῦ τέκνου.

    _____

    _____

35. οὐ λήμψῃ θεὸν ἕως βλέπεις τὰς ἁμαρτίας σου.

    _____

    _____

36. εἶ ὁ φίλος μου καὶ οὐχὶ ἔσῃ ὁ ἐχθρός μου ὅτι θεὸς δεδόξασται ὑπὸ σοῦ.

    _____

    _____

37. ὁ ἅγιος ἄνθρωπος οὐ γινώσκεται ὑπὸ τοῦ κόσμου ὅτι ὁ κόσμος οὐ πεπίστευκεν ἐν θεῷ.

_____

_____

38. ὁ τελώνης οὐ λογίζεται τὰς προσευχὰς τῶν ἐκκλησιῶν· διὸ οὐκέτι ἔρχεται εἰς αὐτάς.

_____

_____

39. οἱ ἀπόστολοι εἶπον ὅτι εἴληφας παρρησίαν διὰ τὴν διδαχὴν Ἰησοῦ Χριστοῦ, καὶ προσεύξομαι ὑπὲρ τῆς παρρησίας σου.

_____

_____

40. ὁ νόμος τῆς ἁμαρτίας γέγραπται ἐπὶ ταῖς καρδίαις τῶν υἱῶν τῆς γῆς, ἀλλὰ μαθήσομαι κατὰ τῶν ἔργων τοῦ διαβόλου.

_____

_____

ENGLISH to GREEK

Provide the Greek translation for each English sentence.

1. The messengers themselves will see the glory of heaven, and they are being seen by the Lord.

_____

_____

2. The master has loosed his servants for himself.

_____

_____

3. Because of the truth, you will now be a faithful woman.

_____

_____

4. We will baptize ourselves in the church, but the strong woman herself has baptized the children in the temple.

_____

_____

5. Both the ministers and the servants of God have been thrown out of the temple by the bad crowds.

_____

_____

6. I was learning the commandments in the Scriptures, but I have been saved by the words of Christ.

_____

_____

7. The good woman is preaching the gospel, but she herself will not believe that I am becoming a disciple of God.

_____

_____

8. The blind men have been healed by the Christ, and the boats have been prepared for Him by the servants of the blind men.

_____

_____

9. The demons have not been thrown into the wilderness by the disciples.

_____

_____

10. My master will be your (sg.) servant, and his work will be a gift to you.

_____

_____

14

IMPERFECT MIDDLE AND PASSIVE, AORIST MIDDLE, AND PLUPERFECT MIDDLE AND PASSIVE INDICATIVE

MATCHING

Choose the best answer.

___ 1. ἐλύετο

    A. Imperfect Passive Indicative, 1st person Plural

___ 2. ἐψεύσω

    B. Present Middle Indicative, 3rd person Singular

___ 3. ἐφερόμεθα

    C. Future Middle Indicative, 2nd person Singular

___ 4. ἐγέγραπτο

    D. Imperfect Passive Indicative, 3rd person Singular

___ 5. ἀκούσῃ

    E. Imperfect Active Indicative, 3rd person Plural

___ 6. εἴρηνται

    F. Future Indicative, 3rd person Singular

___ 7. ἔσται

    G. Aorist Middle Indicative, 2nd person Singular

___ 8. βαπτίζονται

    H. Pluperfect Passive Indicative, 3rd person Singular

___ 9. γίνεται

    I. Present Passive Indicative, 3rd person Plural

___ 10. εἶχον

    J. Perfect Passive Indicative, 3rd person Plural

MULTIPLE CHOICE

Choose the best answer.

____ 1. Which of the following verbs does NOT take secondary middle suffixes?

A. imperfect mid.   B. perfect mid.   C. imperfect pass.   D. pluperfect mid./pass.

____ 2. The imperfect middle and passive indicative is formed on the _____ stem of the verb.

A. present   B. future   C. imperfect active   D. none of the above

____ 3. The technical term for the "ϵ" added to the beginning of the verb is _____.

A. aoristic aspect morpheme   B. neutral morpheme   C. augment   D. allomorph

____ 4. The first aorist middle indicative is formed on the _____ stem of the verb.

A. present   B. future   C. 1ˢᵗ aorist active   D. none of the above

____ 5. In the Greek word ἐλύετο, the letters λυ represent the _____.

A. lexical morpheme   B. past time morpheme   C. person-number suffix   D. neutral morpheme

____ 6. In the Greek word ἐλύετο, the letters το represent the _____.

A. lexical morpheme   B. past time morpheme   C. person-number suffix   D. neutral morpheme

____ 7. In the Greek word ἐλύετο, the first letter ϵ represents the _____.

A. lexical morpheme   B. past time morpheme   C. person-number suffix   D. neutral morpheme

____ 8. In the Greek word ἐλύετο, the second letter ϵ represents the _____.

A. lexical morpheme   B. past time morpheme   C. person-number suffix   D. neutral morpheme

____ 9. In the Greek word ἐργάσασθε, the letters σα represent the _____.

A. aoristic aspect morpheme   B. past time morpheme   C. case-number suffix   D. neutral morpheme

____ 10. The translation for the Greek word ἐλύετο is

A. "he was being loosed"   B. "he himself was loosing"   C. "he was loosing himself"   D. all of the above

TRUE/FALSE

Indicate whether the statement is true or false.

___ 1. The imperfect indicative shares middle and passive forms.

___ 2. The aorist indicative shares middle and passive forms.

___ 3. The perfect indicative shares middle and passive forms.

___ 4. The pluperfect indicative shares middle and passive forms.

___ 5. The future indicative shares middle and passive forms.

___ 6. The present indicative shares middle and passive forms.

___ 7. Verbs that are deponent in the present tense will also be deponent in the imperfect tense.

___ 8. The imperfect middle and passive forms are identical to the second aorist middle forms with the exception of the stem of the verbs.

___ 9. Pluperfect middle and passive forms take primary active suffixes.

___ 10. The rules of amalgamation only apply when creating a future tense Greek verb form.

GREEK to ENGLISH

Provide the English translation for each Greek sentence.

1. διὸ οἱ ἀγαπητοὶ ἡτοιμάσαντο ὑπὲρ τοῦ κυρίου ἀλλ' οὐχ ἡτοιμάσαντο τοὺς οἴκους αὐτῶν ὑπὲρ αὐτοῦ.

   _____

   _____

2. ἐπορεύετο ἡ σοφὴ εἰς τὴν συναγωγὴν τῶν ὑποκριτῶν ὅτι ἐψεύσατο περὶ τοῦ νόμου τοῖς ἀνθρώποις.

   _____

   _____

3. ἀμὴν ἀμὴν ἐγὼ λέγω σοι, οὐκ ἔρχῃ ἐκείνῳ τῷ τόπῳ ὅτι ἡτοιμάσατο αὐτὸν ὑπὲρ τοῦ διαβόλου καὶ τῶν δαιμονίων αὐτοῦ.

   _____

   _____

4. ἐφερόμεθα ὑπὸ τῶν τέκνων ἐν τῷ οἴκῳ ὅτι εὐηγγελισάμεθα περὶ τῆς ἀγάπης τοῦ θεοῦ.

   _____

   _____

5. ἐβαπτίζετο ὁ ἁμαρτωλὸς ὁ κακὸς ὑπὸ τῶν πονηρῶν προφητῶν, ἀλλ' Ἰησοῦς ἦλθεν κατὰ τὰς ἁγίας γραφάς.

   _____

   _____

6. ἐλογίσατο ὁ στρατιώτης τὴν διαθήκην τὴν καινὴν καὶ ἐλάβετο τὴν ἀγάπην καὶ εἰρήνην τοῦ θεοῦ.

   _____

   _____

7. ἀμὴν ἐγενόμην δίκαιος μαθητής, οὐ δὲ ἐγένου καλὸς νεανίας ὅτι ὁ ἀπόστολος ἐβέβλητο ἐκ τοῦ ἱεροῦ.

   _____

   _____

8. οὐκ ἐδεξάμεθα σταυρὸν ἀλλ᾽ ἐφερόμεθα τὸ δυνατὸν εὐαγγέλιον τοῦ θεοῦ ἡμῶν.

   _____

   _____

9. κύριος τῆς δόξης ἐπείθετο ὑπὸ τῶν προφητῶν ἐν τῇ γῇ, ἀλλ᾽ οὐκ προσηυξάμην ἐκείνους τοὺς λόγους ζωῆς.

   _____

   _____

10. βέβληται ἐκ τοῦ ἱεροῦ ὑπὸ τῶν στρατιωτῶν διὰ τὴν ἁμαρτίαν σου;

    _____

    _____

11. βλέψῃ τὸν Χριστὸν ὅτι ἐβλέποντο τὴν δόξαν τοῦ θεοῦ ἐν τοῖς οὐρανοῖς.

    _____

    _____

12. εὐθὺς οἱ φίλοι ἐδέξαντο εἰρήνην, οἱ δὲ μαθηταὶ οὐ φάγονται τὰς ἐπιστολὰς τῆς ζωῆς.

    _____

    _____

13. ἐπορεύεσθε εἰς τοὺς ἀγρούς, ἐπορευόμην δὲ τοῖς οἴκοις τῶν τέκνων τοῦ θεοῦ.

    _____

    _____

14. ἐδίδασκεν ὁ κόσμος τὰς ἀληθείας τοῦ θεοῦ ἐν ταῖς ἁγίαις γραφαῖς.

    _____

    _____

15. ἦρξαν οἱ ὄχλοι τοὺς διακόνους ἐν ταῖς ἐκκλησίαις, ἀλλ᾽ αὐτοὶ οὐκ ἦλθον εἰς τὰς ἐκκλησίας.

    _____

    _____

16. ἐκεῖ ἐβαπτίζοντο οἱ μαθηταὶ παρὰ τὴν θάλασσαν ὑπὸ τοῦ προφήτου ὅτι
    ἐθεραπεύοντο ὑπὸ τοῦ κυρίου.

    _____

    _____

17. πάντοτε δεδόξασται ἡ πιστὴ τὸν σταυρὸν τοῦ Χριστοῦ ὅτι αὐτὸς πέπονθεν ὑπὲρ
    σοῦ.

    _____

    _____

18. ἐδεξάμην λόγους εἰρήνης παρὰ τοῦ δικαίου νεανίου ὅτι αὐτὸς ἔσχεν τὴν
    ἀγάπην τοῦ θεοῦ ἐν τῇ καρδίᾳ αὐτοῦ.

    _____

    _____

19. ὁ νόμος τῆς ζωῆς ἐπείθετο ὑφ' ἑκάστου οἴκου καὶ ἐσῴζετο ὑπὸ θεοῦ.

    _____

    _____

20. ἐδέξασθε τὰ δῶρά μου σὺν χαρᾷ, καὶ προσηυξάμην ὑπὲρ τῶν παιδίων ὑμῶν καὶ
    τῶν φίλων ὑμῶν.

    _____

    _____

21. γέγραπται ὁ πιστὸς διάκονος τὰς ἀληθείας τοῦ λόγου τοῦ θεοῦ, ἀλλ' ὁ διάβολος
    καὶ τὰ δαιμόνια αὐτοῦ οὐκ ἐπεποίθεισαν ἐν αὐταῖς.

    _____

    _____

22. ἐλογίσαντο οἱ νεανίαι καὶ τοὺς νόμους καὶ τὰς διαθήκας ἐν ταῖς συναγωγαῖς
    ταῖς καιναῖς.

    _____

    _____

23. οὐκ ἐλύετο ὁ δοῦλος ὑπὸ τῶν κυρίων αὐτοῦ ὅτι ἐγὼ εἶπον ὅτι γίνεται πονηρὸς δοῦλος.

_____

_____

24. ἐψεύσαντο οἱ κακοὶ ἄνθρωποι περὶ τῆς χαρᾶς τοῦ σταυροῦ, ἀλλ᾽ αὕτη οὐκ ἐψεύσατο περὶ τῆς δόξης τοῦ Χριστοῦ.

_____

_____

25. ἠσπάσαντο οἱ καινοὶ τὰ τέκνα ἐν τῷ οἴκῳ ὅτι οἱ ἰσχυροὶ καὶ πονηροὶ ἦσαν ἔξω ἐν τῇ ἐρήμῳ.

_____

_____

26. οὐκ ἦλθεν ὁ ἀμνὸς τοῦ θεοῦ τῷ ἱερῷ σὺν ὀργῇ, ἀλλ᾽ αὐτὸς οὐκ ἐψεύσατο περὶ αἰωνίου σωτηρίας καὶ αἰωνίου θανάτου.

_____

_____

27. ὧδε ἐθεραπεύετο ὁ μικρὸς τυφλὸς ὑπὸ τῶν προφητῶν ὅτι ὁ κύριος ἀγαθός.

_____

_____

28. ὁ τελώνης οὐκ ἔστιν μικρὸς ἄνθρωπος ὅτι ἐβέβλητο ἐκ τοῦ ναοῦ ὑπὸ τῶν ἰσχυρῶν στρατιωτῶν.

_____

_____

29. εὐθὺς ἐδίδαξα κακὰ ὅτι εἰσῆλθον εἰς κακὸν ἱερόν.

_____

_____

30. ψεύδῃ ὅτε λέγεις ὅτι ἐπείθοντο εἰς θεόν.

_____

_____

31. ἐξήρχοντο ἐκ τῶν πονηρῶν ἱερῶν ὅτι ἐγένοντο ἄνθρωποι θεοῦ.

_____

_____

32. ἐλογίσω τὴν ὁδὸν τοῦ κυρίου, καὶ ἠκούετο αὐτήν.

_____

_____

33. ἡ ἰσχυρὰ ἐπείθετο τὸν λόγον τῆς ἀληθείας, καὶ ἐπεγέγραπτο ἐπὶ λίθοις ὑπὸ τῶν τέκνων τῶν ἀγαθῶν.

_____

_____

34. οὐκ ἐλάβοντο δόξαν ὑπὲρ τῶν λόγων ὑμῶν ὅτι ἤγεσθε τοὺς ὄχλους ὑπὲρ τῆς δόξης.

_____

_____

35. εὐγγελισάμην περὶ τοῦ θεοῦ μου ὅτι ἐσῴζοντο ἀπὸ τῆς ἁμαρτίας αὐτῶν.

_____

_____

36. ἐβούλετο ὅτι ὁ θεὸς οὐκ ἠκούετο τοὺς λόγους σου ὅτι ἡ καρδία σου ἦν πονηρά.

_____

_____

37. σήμερον ἐγένου δοῦλον ὑπὲρ τῆς δόξης τοῦ θεοῦ ὅτι προσηύξω τῷ αὐτῷ θεῷ.

_____

_____

38. ἐγενόμην ἐκεῖνα ὅτι ἐγὼ ἐψευσάμην, ἀλλὰ σὺ εἶπες κακὸν λόγον ἐν τῷ ἱερῷ.

    _____

    _____

39. πεπόνθασιν ἐν τῷ οἴκῳ τῶν πονηρῶν ἀνθρώπων, καὶ ἦλθες μετὰ ἐκείνους τοὺς ἀνθρώπους.

    _____

    _____

40. ἡ χαρὰ τοῦ κυρίου ἐλογίζετο ἐν τῷ κόσμῳ, καὶ οἱ λαοὶ ἐσώζοντο ταῖς ἀληθείαις τοῦ εὐαγγελίου.

    _____

    _____

ENGLISH to GREEK

Provide the Greek translation for each English sentence.

1. The word of the Lord was being written upon the hearts of the sons of men.

   _____

   _____

2. I myself had loosed my servant, but I myself was not preaching about the love of God to him.

   _____

   _____

3. Jesus himself left the glories of heaven, and He became a man.

   _____

   _____

4. You (sg.) were lying because you said that I myself saw the Lord.

   _____

   _____

5.   They had been healed by the good prophet, and they themselves healed their children.

_____

_____

6.   The devil and his demons were not going into the holy temple.

_____

_____

7.   We ourselves have been healed by God, and you (pl.) yourselves will hear from Him.

_____

_____

8.   Were you being heard by the Lord because of your good life?

_____

_____

9.   The Lord was near, but you (sg.) yourself fled from His voice.

_____

_____

10.   We were being led by the good prophets, but you (sg.) did not believe the truths of Christ for yourself.

_____

_____

15

AORIST AND FUTURE PASSIVE INDICATIVE

MATCHING

Choose the best answer.

___ 1. ἐλύθησαν	A.	Aorist Passive Indicative, 3rd person Plural
___ 2. σωθήσῃ	B.	Aorist Passive Indicative, 2nd person Singular
___ 3. ἐγράφη	C.	Aorist Passive Indicative, 3rd person Singular
___ 4. ἐγένου	D.	Pluperfect Passive Indicative, 3rd person Singular
___ 5. ἤρξαντο	E.	Future Passive Indicative, 2nd person Singular
___ 6. ἐγέγραπτο	F.	Future Passive Indicative, 1st person Singular
___ 7. φάγῃ	G.	Aorist Middle Indicative, 3rd person Plural
___ 8. ἐλήμφθης	H.	Future Passive Indicative, 3rd person Plural
___ 9. σωθήσομαι	I.	Aorist Middle Indicative, 2nd person Singular
___ 10. γραφήσονται	J.	Future Middle Indicative, 2nd person Singular

MULTIPLE CHOICE

Choose the best answer.

____ 1. The aorist passive indicative is formed on the _____ stem of the verb.

    A. present   B. aorist active   C. aorist passive   D. none of the above

____ 2. The future passive indicative is formed on the _____ stem of the verb.

    A. future   B. aorist active   C. aorist passive   D. none of the above

____ 3. In the Greek word ἐλύθησαν, the letter ε represents the _____.

    A. augment   B. passive voice morpheme   C. secondary active suffix   D. none of the above

____ 4. In the Greek word ἐλύθησαν, the letters θη represents the _____.

    A. augment   B. passive voice morpheme   C. secondary active suffix   D. none of the above

____ 5. In the Greek word ἐλύθησαν, the letters σαν represent the _____.

    A. augment   B. passive voice morpheme   C. secondary active suffix   D. none of the above

____ 6. _____ Greek verbs in the second aorist passive will include θη in their forms.

    A. All   B. The majority of   C. No   D. none of the above

____ 7. The forms for the future passive indicative are obtained from the _____ principal part.

    A. third   B. fourth   C. fifth   D. sixth

____ 8. The source of the Greek word ἤχθην is _____.

    A. ἔχω   B. ἄγω   C. εἰμί   D. φέρω

____ 9. The tense of the Greek word ἤχθην is _____.

    A. future   B. imperfect   C. first aorist   D. second aorist

____ 10. The voice of the Greek word ἤχθην is _____.

    A. active   B. deponent   C. middle   D. passive

TRUE/FALSE

Indicate whether the statement is true or false.

____ 1. The passive aorist can be broken down into both first and second aorist.

____ 2. The first person singular form of the aorist passive utilizes the fifth principal part.

____ 3. The aorist passive indicative expresses undefined action received by the subject in past time.

____ 4. The subject of the sentence will determine whether a verb takes first or second aorist forms.

____ 5. The forms of the future passive indicative derive from the sixth principal part.

____ 6. The future passive indicative expresses action received by the subject in present time.

____ 7. Context and usage alone will determine whether the kind of action in the future passive is aoristic or imperfective.

____ 8. The addition of θε (θη) to the stem of a verb will not cause any changes to any verb stem.

____ 9. Amalgamation will always occur when creating any first aorist verb form.

____10. Amalgamation will always occur when creating any future verb form.

GREEK to ENGLISH

Provide the English translation for each Greek sentence.

1. ἐκεῖνοι οἱ λόγοι τῆς ὀργῆς ἠκούσθησαν περὶ τοὺς ναοὺς τῶν ὑποκριτῶν διὰ τοῦ πονηροῦ διαβόλου καὶ τῶν δαιμονίων αὐτοῦ.

   _____

   _____

2. καρδίαι ἁμαρτίας λυθήσονται ἐν ἡμέρᾳ σωτηρίας ἐν τῇ ἀληθείᾳ.

   _____

   _____

3. οὐκ ἐπείσθη ἡ δόξα τοῦ Χριστοῦ ὑπὸ τῶν ἀποστόλων τῶν ἀπίστων, καὶ οὐ πιστεύσουσιν τὴν διδαχὴν αὐτῶν.

   _____

   _____

4. οἱ κύριοι ἤχθησαν ὑπὸ τῶν δούλων αὐτῶν εἰς τὴν ἔρημον καὶ ἐδίδαξαν τὴν ἀλήθειαν αὐτοῖς.

   _____

   _____

5. ἡτοιμάσθη τὰ ἔργα τῶν φίλων ἀπὸ τῆς ἀρχῆς ὑπὸ τοῦ κυρίου καὶ τῶν ἀγγέλων αὐτοῦ.

   _____

   _____

6. βληθήσεται ὁ ἔσχατος νόμος ἐκ τῶν ἐκκλησιῶν ὑπὸ τῆς καινῆς διαθήκης.

   _____

   _____

7. ἐδιδάχθητε ὑπὸ τῶν μικρῶν τέκνων περὶ τῶν ἐντολῶν καὶ τῆς ἁμαρτίας.

   _____

   _____

8. ἡ ὑπομονὴ τοῦ μόνου θεοῦ κηρυχθήσεται ὑπὸ τοῦ υἱοῦ τοῦ ἀνθρώπου ἐν τῷ ἱερῷ.

_____

_____

9. ἐσώθησαν οἱ ὄχλοι ἐν ταῖς οἰκίαις, ἀλλ᾽ αὐτοὶ ἔσχον φόβον διὰ τοὺς λόγους τοῦ διαβόλου καὶ τῶν δαιμονίων αὐτοῦ.

_____

_____

10. ἐβαπτίσθημεν εἰς τὴν ἀγάπην τοῦ Χριστοῦ διὰ Πέτρου καὶ τῶν ἄλλων μαθητῶν.

_____

_____

11. ἀκουσθήσῃ ὑπὸ καὶ τῶν ἐξουσιῶν καὶ τῶν κεφαλῶν τῶν ἐκκλησιῶν διὰ τοὺς λόγους ἡμῶν τῆς ὀργῆς.

_____

_____

12. οἱ προφῆται τῆς παρρησίας ἀπεστάλησαν ὑπὸ θεοῦ εἰς τὸν κόσμον κατὰ τὴν ἀλήθειαν τῶν γραφῶν.

_____

_____

13. οὐκ ἐκηρύχθη τὸ εὐαγγέλιον ὑπὸ τοῦ λαοῦ τοῖς ὄχλοις.

_____

_____

14. δοξασθήσεσθε ἐν τῷ καιρῷ ὑμῶν, ἐγὼ δὲ δοξασθήσομαι σήμερον ὑπὸ θεοῦ μου.

_____

_____

15. αἱ ψυχαὶ αἱ ἀγαπηταὶ ἐσώθησαν ὑπὸ τοῦ μόνου θεοῦ.

_____

_____

16. τὰ παιδία τῆς διαθήκης ἐβαπτίσθησαν εἰς τὴν σωτηρίαν διὰ Πέτρου καὶ τῶν ἄλλων μαθητῶν.

_____

_____

17. ἡ ἀλήθεια τῆς γραφῆς ἐγνώσθη ὑφ᾽ ἑκάστου ἀνθρώπου ὅς (who) ἐπίστευσεν ἐν τῇ χαρᾷ τῆς βασιλείας.

_____

_____

18. τὸ δῶρον ἐπέμφθη εἰς τὸν κόσμον ὑπὸ τῶν νεκρῶν νεανιῶν.

_____

_____

19. γραφήσονται αἱ προσευχαὶ αἱ πισταὶ τῶν παιδίων ἐν τῷ βιβλίῳ τῆς ζωῆς ὑπὸ τῶν ἀγγέλων τοῦ θεοῦ.

_____

_____

20. ἐλήμφθη ἡ μαρτυρία τοῦ Πέτρου ὑπὸ τῶν διακονῶν τῶν πιστῶν κατὰ τὸν νόμον τοῦ κόσμου.

_____

_____

21. οἱ υἱοὶ τῶν τυφλῶν εἰσῆλθον εἰς τὸν οἶκον ὑπὲρ τῶν δώρων διὰ τὴν ἀγάπην αὐτῶν ὑπὲρ ἐκείνων τῶν δώρων.

_____

_____

22. ὁ λαὸς σωθήσεται ὑπὸ τῆς διδαχῆς τῆς δικαίας τῆς ζωῆς Χριστοῦ ὅτι ἤκουσαν τὸ εὐαγγέλιον.

_____

_____

23. ἐλύθη ἡ γλῶσσα τοῦ ἀκαθάρτου ἁμαρτωλοῦ ἐν τῷ ἱερῷ ὑπὸ τοῦ φίλου τοῦ
    εὐαγγελίου.

    _____

    _____

24. οὐ πεισθήσονται οἱ λόγοι τοῦ ἐχθροῦ ὑπὸ τῶν δικαίων τέκνων ὅτι πιστεύουσιν
    ἐν Χριστῷ.

    _____

    _____

25. ἡ καρδία μου λίθου ἔσται καλὴ καρδία ὅτι ἐθεραπεύθη ὑπὸ τοῦ υἱοῦ τοῦ θεοῦ.

    _____

    _____

26. γνωσθήσονται καὶ ἡ ἡμέρα καὶ ἡ ὥρα τοῦ κυρίου ὑφ᾽ ἑκάστου ἀνθρώπου καὶ
    ἑκάστου παιδίου;

    _____

    _____

27. τὰ παιδία τοῦ προφήτου ἤχθη εἰς τὴν δικαιοσύνην τοῦ Χριστοῦ διὰ τῶν
    μαθητῶν αὐτοῦ.

    _____

    _____

28. ὁ Χριστὸς ὁ ἅγιος ἐδοξάσθη ἐν τοῖς οἴκοις ὑπὸ καὶ τῶν μαθητῶν αὐτοῦ καὶ τῶν
    ἀδελφῶν αὐτοῦ.

    _____

    _____

29. λημφθήσονται εἰς τὸν οἶκον τοῦ θεοῦ ὑπὸ τῶν ἀδελφῶν.

    _____

    _____

30. ἐπέμφθη ὁ θεὸς τοῦ οὐρανοῦ εἰς τοῦτον τὸν κόσμον ὑπὲρ τῆς σωτηρίας ἀνθρώπων.

_____

_____

31. ἐλήμφθης εἰς τοὺς ἀγροὺς τοὺς κακοὺς ὑπὸ τῆς κεφαλῆς τοῦ πονηροῦ ἱεροῦ;

_____

_____

32. τὰ ἀγαθὰ ἔργα τῶν μαθητῶν ὤφθησαν ὑπὸ τῶν ὀφθαλμῶν τοῦ ὄχλου;

_____

_____

33. αἱ παραβολαὶ τοῦ ἄρτου ἐδιδάχθησαν τοῖς διακόνοις τῆς εἰρήνης ὑπὸ τῶν ἰσχυρῶν ἀγγέλων τοῦ θεοῦ.

_____

_____

34. οἱ πονηροὶ ἄγγελοι ἐγένοντο δαιμόνια ὅτι αἱ πονηραὶ ἐπιθυμίαι αὐτῶν ὤφθησαν ὑπὸ θεοῦ.

_____

_____

35. ἐβλήθη ὁ ἀκάθαρτος ἄγγελος ἐκ οὐρανοῦ καὶ ὁ θρόνος τοῦ θεοῦ ἐδοξάσθη ὑπὸ τῶν ἀγγέλων ἐν οὐρανῷ.

_____

_____

36. ἑτοιμασθήσεται ἡ συναγωγὴ προσευχῆς, καὶ ἡ φωνὴ τοῦ θεοῦ ἠκούσθη ὑπὸ τῶν τέκνων αὐτοῦ.

_____

_____

37. πιστευθήσονται ὑπὸ τοῦ Πέτρου διὰ τὴν ἀγάπην ὑμῶν ὑπὲρ τῶν ἀδελφῶν.

     _____

     _____

38. ἐγράφη ἡ μαρτυρία τῶν μαθητῶν καὶ τῶν ἀποστόλων ὑπὲρ τῶν ἐκκλησιῶν τῆς ζωῆς ὑπὸ τοῦ ἀξίου νεανίου.

     _____

     _____

39. ἐκεῖνος ὁ θεὸς λίθου ἐπέμφθη εἰς τὴν θάλασσαν ὑπὸ τοῦ δικαίου καὶ σοφοῦ δούλου τοῦ Χριστοῦ.

     _____

     _____

40. ὁ σταυρὸς τοῦ Χριστοῦ ἐγενήθη σημεῖον τῷ κόσμῳ ὅτι ὁ Χριστὸς ἐπορεύθη πρὸς τὸν σταυρὸν διὰ τὴν ἀγάπην αὐτοῦ ὑπὲρ τῶν λαῶν τοῦ κόσμου.

     _____

     _____

ENGLISH to GREEK

Provide the Greek translation for each English sentence.

1. The good children were led into the wilderness by the faithful minister.

     _____

     _____

2. The children of God went into the churches, and they were preaching the truth.

     _____

     _____

3. The sinners in the world will be saved by the powerful glory of the Lord.

     _____

     _____

4. The Son of God became the Son of Man, and He Himself saves the world from sin.

_____

_____

5. The words of the beloved apostle will be written by the wise young man.

_____

_____

6. Were those teachings of the prophets heard in the synagogues by the crowds?

_____

_____

7. The glory of the Lord was seen beside the road by the unbelieving sinner.

_____

_____

8. The gospel of Jesus Christ will be preached by the small children in the fields.

_____

_____

9. The same demons were sent into the world, but I myself will not believe their teachings.

_____

_____

10. The servants of the soldiers will be taught the word of God by the ministers.

_____

_____

16

Review of the Indicative Mood

MATCHING

Match each term with the most appropriate option.

___ 1. lexical morpheme

___ 2. inflectional morpheme

___ 3. past time morpheme

___ 4. passive voice morpheme

___ 5. future time morpheme

___ 6. aoristic aspect morpheme

___ 7. perfective aspect morpheme

___ 8. verb root

___ 9. neutral morpheme

___ 10. imperfective aspect morpheme

___ 11. final morpheme

___ 12. multiple morpheme

A. θε (θη)

B. σα

C. σ

D. a morpheme that conveys information about the word's grammatical meaning

E. basic nucleus upon which all the other verb forms of that verb are based (may not be identical with the lexical morpheme)

F. a morpheme that is added to a verb inherently aoristic when an imperfective form is required

G. ε or ο

H. a morpheme that conveys multiple information

I. verb stem that carries the fundamental meaning of the word

J. κα

K. indicates that the action of the verb refers to past time

L. usually the person-number suffix

MULTIPLE CHOICE

Choose the best answer.

____ 1. Which of the following represents the syllabic augment?

    A. ἤκουον   B. ἔλυον   C. εἰρήνευον   D. none

____ 2. Which of the following represents the temporal augment?

    A. ἤκουον   B. ἔλυον   C. εἰρήνευον   D. none

____ 3. Which of the following represents the zero augment?

    A. ἤκουον   B. ἔλυον   C. εἰρήνευον   D. none

____ 4. Which of the following English phrases is classified as imperfect passive indicative?

    A. I was loosing   B. I was loosed   C. I was being loosed   D. I was loosing myself

____ 5. Which of the following English phrases is classified as future passive indicative?

    A. I will be loosed   B. I will loose   C. I have loosed   D. I will loose myself

____ 6. The verb εὐηγγελισάμην indicates which tense?

    A. future   B. first aorist   C. imperfect   D. second aorist

____ 7. The verb εὐηγγελισάμην indicates which voice?

    A. active   B. middle   C. passive

____ 8. The verb σωθήσομαι indicates which tense?

    A. present   B. first aorist   C. imperfect   D. future

____ 9. The verb σωθήσομαι indicates which voice?

    A. active   B. middle   C. passive

____ 10. Which form represents the imperfect indicative of εἰμί?

    A. ἐστέ   B. ἔσται   C. ἦσαν   D. ἔσῃ

TRUE/FALSE

Indicate whether the statement is true or false.

___ 1. The identification of the morphemes in any given form of a Greek verb is termed *morphological analysis.*

___ 2. The lexical morpheme of a verb is always a "bound" form because it is able to exist without a grammatical morpheme attached to it.

___ 3. The lexical morpheme is inherently either imperfective or aoristic.

___ 4. The morpheme is the only purely temporal element in the Greek verb system.

___ 5. Perfective reduplication usually involves the repetition of the initial consonant of the verb stem plus the vowel α.

___ 6. The morpheme κα can be found only in the active voice.

___ 7. Person-number suffixes normally also indicate mood.

___ 8. There are eight categories of morphemes that can occur in the indicative verb.

___ 9. If a verb lacks a past time morpheme, it is either present, future, or perfect.

___ 10. If a verb has both the past time morpheme and the aoristic aspect morpheme, it is a second aorist.

17

NOUNS OF THE THIRD DECLENSION

MATCHING

Choose the best answer.

____ 1. declension

A. decides the function of a noun (i.e., subject, direct object, etc.)

____ 2. case form

B. $\psi\iota(\nu)$

____ 3. gender

C. $\alpha\sigma\iota(\nu)$

____ 4. $\pi, \beta, \phi + \sigma\iota(\nu) =$

D. indicates whether a part of speech is masculine, feminine, or neuter

____ 5. $\kappa, \gamma, \chi + \sigma\iota(\nu) =$

E. $\xi\iota(\nu)$

____ 6. $\tau, \delta, \theta + \sigma\iota(\nu) =$

F. the inflection of a noun

____ 7. $\alpha\nu\tau + \sigma\iota(\nu) =$

G. $ου\sigma\iota(\nu)$

____ 8. $ο\nu\tau + \sigma\iota(\nu) =$

H. $\sigma\iota(\nu)$

MULTIPLE CHOICE

Choose the best answer.

___ 1. One can assume that the stems of most third declension nouns will be most easily recognizable in their _____ singular case.

A. nominative   B. genitive   C. dative   D. accusative

___ 2. The genitive singular form of third declension nouns always ends in _____.

A. ο   B. ι   C. ς   D. ας

___ 3. The dative singular form of third declension nouns always ends in _____.

A. ο   B. ι   C. ς   D. ας

___ 4. The nominative and accusative plural forms of third declension nouns always end in _____.

A. ο   B. ι   C. ς   D. σι

___ 5. The genitive plural form of third declension nouns always ends in _____.

A. ων   B. ι   C. ς   D. σι

___ 6. The dative plural form of third declension nouns always ends in _____.

A. ων   B. ι   C. ς   D. σι

___ 7. Which is not a parsing element for nouns?

A. part of speech   B. voice   C. number   D. source

TRUE/FALSE

Indicate whether the statement is true or false.

_____ 1. The widest range of paradigms for different stems will be found in the third declension.

_____ 2. The genitive singular ending of third declension nouns is the same as the nominative singular ending of first declension nouns.

_____ 3. The neuter forms for nominative and accusative cases are identical in the third declension.

_____ 4. The genitive plural form of the Greek word for "ruler" is ἄρχων.

_____ 5. The nominative singular form of the Greek word for "body" is σώματος.

_____ 6. The lexical stem for the word "flesh" is σάρξ.

GREEK to ENGLISH

Provide the English translation for each Greek sentence.

1. ὁ στρατιώτης τοῦ βασιλέως ἔλαβεν τὴν παράκλησιν ἀπὸ τοῦ ἁγίου πνεύματος τοῦ θεοῦ.

   _____

   _____

2. ὁ Χριστὸς ἔπαθεν τὸν θάνατον τοῦ σταυροῦ ὅτι ὁ ἀρχιερεὺς καὶ οἱ φίλοι αὐτοῦ οὐκ ἐπίστευσαν εἰς αὐτόν.

   _____

   _____

3. ὁ μάρτυς τῆς ἀληθείας ἔφυγεν εἰς τὴν ἔρημον κατὰ τὸ θέλημα τοῦ θεοῦ.

   _____

   _____

4. οἱ στρατιῶται εὑρίσκουσιν τὸ ὕδωρ ἐν τῇ ἐρήμῳ.

   _____

   _____

5. ἡ κρίσις τοῦ θεοῦ ἐστιν καὶ ἀξία καὶ σοφή.

   _____

   _____

6. ὁ ἄνθρωπος καὶ τὸ σπέρμα αὐτοῦ οὐ βλέψονται τὸ τέλος τῆς ἀγάπης τοῦ θεοῦ.

   _____

   _____

7. ὁ ἄρχων τοῦ ναοῦ καὶ ὁ ἕτερος ἄρχων τῆς συναγωγῆς οὐ πιστεύσουσιν τὴν διδαχὴν τοῦ Χριστοῦ καὶ τῶν μαθητῶν αὐτοῦ.

   _____

   _____

8. ἐβαπτίσθη τὸ σῶμα τοῦ Χριστοῦ εἰς τὴν ἐκκλησίαν διὰ τῶν διακονῶν τῶν πιστῶν τῆς εἰρήνης.

_____

_____

9. Πέτρος, ὁ μαθητὴς τοῦ κυρίου, ἤκουσεν τὴν κλῆσιν τοῦ Χριστοῦ παρὰ τὴν θάλασσαν.

_____

_____

10. Ἰησοῦς Χριστὸς πέμψει τὸν διάβολον καὶ τὰ δαιμόνια αὐτοῦ εἰς τὸ σκότος καὶ θάνατον.

_____

_____

11. ὁ ἀνὴρ ὁ ἀγαπητὸς ἡτοίμασεν τὰ τέκνα αὐτοῦ ὑπὲρ τῆς βασιλείας καὶ τῆς δόξης τοῦ θεοῦ.

_____

_____

12. τὰ στόματα τῶν ἀδελφῶν εἶπον σοφίαν τοῖς παιδίοις τοῖς ἀγαθοῖς διὰ τὴν ἀγάπην αὐτῶν ὑπὲρ αὐτῶν.

_____

_____

13. αἱ γυναῖκες τοῦ λόγου πεπόνθασιν ἰσχυρὰν θλίψιν διὰ τὸν διάβολον τὸν πονηρόν.

_____

_____

14. τὸ ἔλεος τοῦ θεοῦ θεραπεύσει τὸν τυφλὸν τὸν ἀκάθαρτον καὶ τὸν πατέρα αὐτοῦ.

_____

_____

15. ἐδιδάχθησαν περὶ τοῦ αἰῶνος τῆς γῆς ὑπὸ τῶν σοφῶν ἀνθρώπων ἐν τῇ ἐρήμῳ.

_____

_____

16. βλέπουσιν οἱ δοῦλοι οἱ ἰσχυροὶ πῦρ ἐν τοῖς ἀγροῖς αὐτῶν.

_____

_____

17. τὴν δύναμιν τῆς ἀναστάσεως οὐκ ἔγνωμεν ἐν ταῖς καρδίαις ἡμῶν, νῦν δὲ ἡμεῖς μεμαθήκαμεν περὶ τῆς δόξης τοῦ θεοῦ.

_____

_____

18. ἕκαστον μέρος ἐπιστολῆς ἐγράφη ὑπὸ τῶν τέκνων τοῖς ἀπίστοις στρατιώταις ἐν τοῖς ἀγροῖς.

_____

_____

19. οἱ τυφλοὶ ἐθεραπεύοντο ὑπὸ τῆς χειρὸς καὶ τῆς φωνῆς τοῦ Χριστοῦ ἐν τῷ ναῷ.

_____

_____

20. ἡ ἀλήθεια τῶν ῥημάτων αὐτοῦ ἡτοίμασεν τὸν λαὸν ὑπὲρ τῆς ἡμέρας τοῦ κυρίου καὶ τῆς βασιλείας αὐτοῦ.

_____

_____

21. πιστεύω ὅτι ἔχω γνῶσιν καὶ σοφίαν, ἐγὼ δὲ οὐ γινώσκω τὰς ἀληθείας ἐν ταῖς γραφαῖς.

_____

_____

22. τὸ ἔτος τὸ πιστὸν τῆς σωτηρίας ἐκηρύχθη τοῖς λαοῖς τῆς ὁδοῦ ὑπὸ τῶν νεανιῶν.

_____

_____

23. σέσωται τῇ χάριτι τοῦ θεοῦ;

_____

_____

24. τὸ πῦρ τῆς κρίσεως αὐτοῦ λυθήσεται ἀπ᾽ οὐρανοῦ ἐφ᾽ ἡμῖν;

_____

_____

25. ἑώρακα τὴν ἀνάστασιν τοῦ κυρίου ἡμῶν καὶ ἐκηρύξαμεν τὸ εὐαγγέλιον τοῖς ὄχλοις.

_____

_____

26. ὁ ἱερεὺς καὶ ὁ ἀρχιερεὺς τοῦ ναοῦ ἐκήρυσσον περὶ τοῦ ἐλέους τοῦ θεοῦ τοῖς ὄχλοις.

_____

_____

27. αὕτη ἡ σάρξ μου οὐ δοξάζεται ὑπὸ τοῦ θεοῦ τοῦ οὐρανοῦ καὶ τῶν ἀνδρῶν τῆς γῆς.

_____

_____

28. γινώσκει τὸ πνεῦμα τοῦ θεοῦ καὶ τὰς καρδίας τῶν ἀνθρώπων καὶ τὰς προσευχὰς τῶν τέκνων αὐτοῦ.

_____

_____

29. ὁ ἱερεὺς τῆς διαθήκης ἡτοίμασεν τοὺς ἀμνοὺς ὑπὲρ τῆς ὥρας τῆς χαρᾶς.

---

30. ἐσμὲν ἔθνος ἁμαρτωλῶν, ἀλλ᾽ ὁ υἱὸς τοῦ ἀνθρώπου ἐσῴζετο τὸν λαὸν αὐτοῦ ἀφ᾽ ἁμαρτίας αὐτῶν.

---

31. αὕτη ἡ ἡμέρα ἦν ἁγία, αὐτὴ δὲ ἔσται κακὴ νύξ.

---

32. δοξασθήσεται τὸ ὄνομα τοῦ θεοῦ ὑπὸ τῶν φωνῶν τῶν πληθῶν.

---

33. ὁ ἀγαθὸς διάκονος ἐδίδαξεν τὴν ἀλήθειαν τοῖς γραμματεῦσιν, οὐ δὲ ἐπίστευσαν αὐτήν.

---

34. τὸ γένος τῶν ἀνθρώπων σῴζεται ὑπὸ τοῦ υἱοῦ τοῦ θεοῦ, καὶ ἐσμὲν τὸ σπέρμα τοῦ Χριστοῦ.

---

35. ἡ σωτηρία τῶν τυφλῶν ἔπεμψεν ἐλπίδα τοῖς ἰσχυροῖς ὅτι αὐταὶ οὐ οἴδασιν τὴν ἀλήθειαν.

---

36. τὸ θέλημα τοῦ πατρός μού ἐστιν ἀγαθὴ ἐπιθυμία, καὶ γνώσεται τὴν καρδίαν μου καὶ τὰ ἀγαθὰ ἔργα μου.

_____

_____

37. ὁ ἄρχων τοῦ σκότους τούτου τοῦ κόσμου πονηρός.

_____

_____

38. ὁ πατήρ μου τὸ ὄνομα τοῦ Χριστοῦ ἐδόξασεν καὶ ἐν τοῖς οἴκοις καὶ ταῖς συναγωγαῖς.

_____

_____

39. ἐλήμφθη τὸ φῶς τοῦ κόσμου ὑπὸ τῶν ἀκαθάρτων ἁμαρτωλῶν ὅτι ἦμεν φῶτα ἐν τούτῳ τῷ κόσμῳ.

_____

_____

40. τὸ αἷμα τοῦ Χριστοῦ ἐθεραπεύετο ἀνθρώπους ἀφ' ἁμαρτίας καὶ θανάτου.

_____

_____

ENGLISH to GREEK

Provide the Greek translation for each English sentence.

1. Will the faith of my father lead my brother to the Lord?

_____

_____

2. The daughters of the prophets spoke the truths of the Scriptures because they are beloved.

_____

_____

3. The blessed angels of God do not know the power of His resurrection.

    _____

    _____

4. Jesus ate bread because He was flesh and blood.

    _____

    _____

5. The scribes and priests did not preach the same words to their disciples in the different sanctuaries.

    _____

    _____

6. The darkness does not have the light of God, and the slanderer does not know the blood of Christ.

    _____

    _____

7. Will you (pl.) trust in the grace of God instead of your evil flesh?

    _____

    _____

8. The multitude was baptized in the name of the Father, the Son, and the Holy Spirit.

    _____

    _____

9. You (pl.) will be my witnesses, and the nations will hear about the grace, mercy, and peace of God.

    _____

    _____

10. I am the resurrection and the life and the hope of the world.

    _____

    _____

18

ADJECTIVES, PRONOUNS, AND NUMERALS OF THE FIRST AND THIRD DECLENSIONS

MATCHING

Choose the best answer.

___ 1. οὐδείς   A. into

___ 2. εἰς   B. great

___ 3. πολύς   C. -τατος, -η, -ον

___ 4. δώδεκα   D. -τερος, -α, -ον

___ 5. εἷς   E. two

___ 6. μέγας   F. twelve

___ 7. μηδείς   G. no one, nothing (with indicative)

___ 8. comparative ending   H. many, much

___ 9. superlative ending   I. one

___ 10. δύο   J. no one, nothing (with non-indicative)

MULTIPLE CHOICE

Choose the best answer.

___ 1. When πᾶς is used in the predicate position, it usually means "_____."

      A. all   B. whole   C. every   D. one

___ 2. When standing alone, πᾶς usually means "_____."

      A. all   B. whole   C. every   D. every man

___ 3. When πᾶς is used in the attributive position, it usually means "_____."

      A. all   B. whole   C. every   D. one

___ 4. When πᾶς is used with an anarthrous noun, it usually means "_____" in the singular.

      A. all   B. whole   C. every   D. every man

___ 5. The feminine form πᾶσα conforms to which first declension noun?

      A. ἡμέρα   B. δόξα   C. φωνή   D. σάρξ

___ 6. The feminine form of the Greek word for "one" conforms to which first declension noun?

      A. ἡμέρα   B. δόξα   C. φωνή   D. σάρξ

___ 7. The feminine form of πολύς and μέγας conforms to which first declension noun?

      A. ἡμέρα   B. δόξα   C. φωνή   D. σάρξ

___ 8. The superlative of σοφός is _____.

      A. σοφώτερος   B. σοφότατος   C. σοφώτατος   D. none of the above

___ 9. The comparative of ἀγαθός is _____.

      A. ἀγατέρος   B. ἀγατάτος   C. κρείσσων   D. none of the above

___ 10. The comparative of κακός is _____.

      A. χείρων   B. κείρων   C. κρείσων   D. none of the above

TRUE/FALSE

Indicate whether the statement is true or false.

____ 1. Sometimes πᾶς can have the meaning of "full" or "pure" in the New Testament.

____ 2. One way to express a comparison in Greek is to place the noun or pronoun with which the comparison is made in the dative case.

____ 3. Greek comparatives and superlatives are always to be understood as meaning "more of x" and "most of x."

____ 4. At times, the comparative can be used in an elative sense, meaning "very" or "exceedingly."

____ 5. The numeral "one" in Greek takes the rough breathing mark in the masculine and neuter genders.

GREEK to ENGLISH

Provide the English translation for each Greek sentence.

1. ὁ ἄρχων τοῦ ναοῦ καὶ ὁ νεώτερος ἄρχων τῆς συναγωγῆς οὐ πιστεύουσιν τὴν διδαχὴν τοῦ διαβόλου καὶ πολλῶν λόγων αὐτοῦ.

   _____

   _____

2. ὁ προφήτης τῆς εἰρήνης πέμψει πᾶν δαιμόνιον σκότει καὶ θανάτῳ.

   _____

   _____

3. ἐδιδάχθησαν καὶ οἱ ἰσχυρότεροι προφῆται καὶ οἱ δώδεκα μαθηταὶ τὴν γραφὴν ὑπὸ τοῦ πυρὸς τοῦ λόγου αὐτοῦ.

   _____

   _____

4. ὁ δοῦλος τοῦ βασιλέως ἔλαβεν τὴν παράκλησιν πασῶν τῶν πόλεων τοῦ θεοῦ.

   _____

   _____

5. τὴν δύναμιν τῆς ἀναστάσεως οὐκ ἔγνωμεν ἐν πάσαις καρδίαις ἡμῶν, αὐτοὶ δὲ νῦν μεμαθήκασιν περὶ τῆς δόξης τοῦ θεοῦ.

   _____

   _____

6. ὁ ἀγαθὸς διάκονος διδάξει ἕνα ἕκαστον τὴν ἀλήθειαν τοῦ θεοῦ, οὐ δὲ ἀκούσουσιν.

   _____

   _____

7. πολλοὶ οὐ ἐδοξάσθησαν ὑπὸ τοῦ θεοῦ τοῦ οὐρανοῦ ἐν τῇ βασιλείᾳ.

   _____

   _____

8. τὸ πλῆθος τοῦ ἐλέους αὐτοῦ θεραπεύει τὸ πᾶν σῶμα πάσης.

    _____

    _____

9. ὁ μόνος Μεσσίας ἔπαθεν καὶ θάνατον καὶ τὸν σταυρὸν διὰ πᾶν γένος τῆς ἁμαρτίας.

    _____

    _____

10. ἐβαπτίσθη τὸ σῶμα τοῦ Χριστοῦ ἐν τῇ ἐρήμῳ ὑπὸ τῶν διακονῶν τῶν ἀλήθων τῆς χάριτος.

    _____

    _____

11. βλέπεις τὴν ἀληθῆ ἀνάστασιν τοῦ κυρίου ἡμῶν, καὶ κηρύξω τὸ εὐαγγέλιον τοῖς πλήθεσιν τῶν ἀνθρώπων.

    _____

    _____

12. τὸ γένος τῶν ἀνθρώπων τῶν μεγάλων σωθήσεται ὑπὸ τοῦ ἑνὸς υἱοῦ τοῦ θεοῦ καὶ γίνονται τὸ σπέρμα τοῦ Χριστοῦ.

    _____

    _____

13. ἔγνωκεν τὸ ἀληθὲς πνεῦμα τοῦ θεοῦ καὶ τὴν καρδίαν τοῦ ἀνθρώπου καὶ τὴν προσευχὴν αὐτοῦ.

    _____

    _____

14. ἐδιδάχθησαν τὸν αἰῶνα τῆς γῆς ὑπὸ τῶν μεγίστων ἀδελφῶν ἐν τοῖς οἴκοις αὐτῶν.

    _____

    _____

15. οἱ μάρτυρες τῆς ἀναστάσεως ἔφυγεν εἰς τὴν ἔρημον καὶ τῇ θαλάσσῃ κατὰ πάντας.

_____

_____

16. εἷς τῶν ἀδελφῶν εἶπεν τὴν ἀλήθειαν τοῖς παιδίοις τοῖς ἀγαθοῖς διὰ τὴν ἀγάπην αὐτῶν.

_____

_____

17. σοφία πολλῶν προφητῶν αὐτοῦ ἡτοίμασεν τοὺς λαοὺς ὑπὲρ τῆς ἡμέρας τοῦ κυρίου καὶ τῆς βασιλείας αὐτοῦ.

_____

_____

18. ἡ θλῖψις τοῦ Ἰησοῦ θεραπεύει ἕκαστον ἄνθρωπον ἀφ' ἁμαρτίας καὶ θανάτου.

_____

_____

19. πάντα τὰ τέκνα τοῦ κόσμου ἐστιν πονηρότερα ἢ οἱ ἀδελφοί.

_____

_____

20. διάκονος μιᾶς διαθήκης ἡτοίμασεν τοὺς ἀμνοὺς ὑπὲρ τῆς ὥρας τῆς χαρᾶς.

_____

_____

21. σὺ ἔχεις τὴν χάριτα τοῦ θεοῦ καὶ ἐπὶ σὲ καὶ τα πέντε τέκνα σου.

_____

_____

22. ὁ πατὴρ καὶ ἡ μήτηρ, φίλοι κυρίου, ἤκουσαν τὴν φωνὴν τοῦ Χριστοῦ παρὰ πολὺν ὄχλον.

_____

_____

23. ὁ φίλος τοῦ μεγίστου ἡτοίμασεν τὸν λαὸν ὑπὲρ τῆς βασιλείας καὶ τῆς δόξης τοῦ θεοῦ.

_____

_____

24. οἱ δύο εὑρίσκουσι τὸν ἄρτον ἐν τῇ ἐρήμῳ ἐπὶ τὴν ὁδόν.

_____

_____

25. αἱ γυναῖκες τοῦ φόβου πεπόνθασιν μεγάλην θλῖψιν διὰ τὸν ἕνα διάβολον.

_____

_____

26. αἱ ἀληθεῖς κρίσεις τοῦ Χριστοῦ εἰσιν καὶ ἅγιαι καὶ σοφαί.

_____

_____

27. καὶ οἱ ἀδελφοὶ καὶ οἱ ἱερεῖς τοῦ ναοῦ τοῦ μεγάλου κηρύσσουσιν τὰ ἐλέη τοῦ θεοῦ καὶ τοῦ Χριστοῦ αὐτοῦ τοῖς ὄχλοις.

_____

_____

28. ἡ σωτηρία πάντων τῶν τυφλῶν ἔπεμψεν ἐλπίδα τοῖς ἀποστόλοις ὅτι οὐ γινώσκουσι τὴν χαρὰν τοῦ Χριστοῦ.

_____

_____

29. ἐλήμφθη ἐν τῷ φωτὶ τοῦ σταυροῦ ἅπας τῶν ἀκαθάρτων τῶν ἁμαρτωλῶν ἐν τοῖς πονηροῖς τοῖς οἴκοις.

   _____

   _____

30. δοξασθήσεται οἱ λόγοι τοῦ θεοῦ ὑπὸ τῶν νεανιῶν παρὰ ταῖς φωναῖς ἡμῶν.

   _____

   _____

31. οἱ δύο ὑποκριταὶ λυθήσονται ὑπὸ τῆς χειρὸς καὶ τῆς ἀληθοῦς φωνῆς τοῦ Χριστοῦ ἐν τῷ ναῷ.

   _____

   _____

32. Ἀβραὰμ καὶ πάντα τὸ σπέρμα αὐτοῦ οὐ γινώσκουσι τὸ τέλος τῆς ἀγάπης τοῦ θεοῦ.

   _____

   _____

33. τὸ παιδίον ἔγραψεν πᾶν μέρος τῆς ἐπιστολῆς τοῖς δικαιοτάτοις διακόνοις τοῦ λόγου.

   _____

   _____

34. οἱ δοῦλοι οἱ πιστοὶ ἐξέβαλον τὰ σπέρματα τὰ καινὰ ὑπὲρ τοῦ ἔργου ἐν τοῖς ἀγροῖς.

   _____

   _____

35. ἔχω τὴν γνῶσιν καὶ τὴν σοφίαν, ἐγὼ δὲ ἔχω οὐδὲν τῆς ἀληθείας τῆς γραφῆς ἐν τῇ καρδίᾳ μου.

   _____

   _____

36. ἐσμὲν ἔθνος μιᾶς γλώσσης, ἀλλ’ ὁ υἱὸς τοῦ ἀνθρώπου σῴζει τὸν λαὸν αὐτοῦ ἐν τοῖς τόποις τοῖς πολλοῖς.

_____

_____

37. ὁ πατὴρ τοῦ οὐρανοῦ ἀληθοῦς τὸ ὄνομα τοῦ Χριστοῦ ἐδόξασεν ἐν καὶ τοῖς οἴκοις καὶ ταῖς συναγωγαῖς.

_____

_____

38. τὸ ἔτος τὸ καλὸν τῆς βασιλείας λέγεται ὑπὸ πολλῶν τῶν νεανιῶν τοῖς λαοῖς τῆς ἐρήμου.

_____

_____

39. τὸ θέλημα τοῦ πατρὸς τοῦ μεγάλου μού ἐστιν ἀγαθὴ καὶ ἀληθὴς ἐπιθυμία, καὶ γινώσκει τὴν καρδίαν μου καὶ τὰ ἔργα μου.

_____

_____

40. αὕτη ἡ ἡμέρα ἡ μεγάλη ἐστὶν ἡ ἀληθής, αὕτη δέ ἐστιν νὺξ θανάτου.

_____

_____

ENGLISH TO GREEK

Provide the Greek translation for each English sentence.

1. The second witness preached the two covenants of Christ both in the day and night.

_____

_____

2. Every woman was baptized in the one name of the Father, the Son, and the Spirit.

_____

_____

3. The darkness does not have the true light of God, and the slanderer does not know anything about the blood of Christ.

    _____

    _____

4. Jesus ate more bread because of His flesh.

    _____

    _____

5. All the daughters of the father speak the truth of Scripture, and they are beloved.

    _____

    _____

6. The holiest scribes and priests preached the word to the peoples in the temple.

    _____

    _____

7. The true faith of my four brothers leads the hypocrites to the Lord.

    _____

    _____

8. The worthiest angels of God did not know the power of His resurrection.

    _____

    _____

9. Do you (pl.) trust in the grace of the whole cross for your sins?

    _____

    _____

10. The greatest cities of the Gentiles have not prepared their children for the king.

    _____

    _____

19

CONTRACT AND LIQUID VERBS

MATCHING

Choose the best answer.

____ 1. contraction

____ 2. asigmatic aorist

____ 3. α + E-sound (ε, η)

____ 4. φιλῶ

____ 5. α + any combination with ι

____ 6. ε + ε

____ 7. ε + o

____ 8. ε + any long vowel/diphthong

____ 9. φιλέω

____ 10. o + any combination with ι

A. does not contain the usual σ

B. ει

C. two vowels combine to form either a long vowel or a diphthong

D. the Greek word for "I love" prior to applying the rules of contraction

E. the Greek word for "I love" after applying the rules of contraction

F. ου

G. οι

H. α

I. ε drops out

J. ᾳ

MULTIPLE CHOICE

Choose the best answer.

____ 1. Which vowel is not a short vowel?

    A. α   B. η   C. ε   D. o

____ 2. There are _____ rules of contraction.

    A. five   B. six   C. eight   D. nine

____ 3. In which tense does contraction NOT occur?

    A. present   B. aorist   C. imperfect   D. none of the above

____ 4. Which of these is not considered a liquid consonant?

    A. μ   B. ρ   C. σ   D. λ

____ 5. The future form of μένω is _____.

    A. μενῶ   B. μένσω   C. μένεσω   D. none of the above

____ 6. The first aorist form of ἐγείρω is _____.

    A. ἤγειρσα   B. ἤγειρα   C. ἤγερσα   D. there is no first aorist form

____ 7. What are the person and number of the verb δικαιοῖ?

    A. 1st singular   B. 2nd singular   C. 3rd plural   D. 3rd singular

____ 8. The present active indicative, first person singular form of ζάω is _____.

    A. ζαῶν   B. ζῶν   C. ζῶ   D. none of the above

____ 9. Complete the rule of contraction: α + O sound (o, ω, ου) = _____.

    A. ου   B. ω   C. η   D. ει

____10. Complete the rule of contraction: o + any combination of ι = _____.

    A. οι   B. ου   C. ω   D. o drops out

TRUE/FALSE

Indicate whether the statement is true or false.

_____ 1. When parsing any inflected form of a contract verb, it is common to cite the uncontract-ed form of a contract verb as the source.

_____ 2. A contract verb can be found in the Greek New Testament in its uncontracted form.

_____ 3. Verbs whose stem ends in λ, μ, ν, or ρ are called contract verbs.

_____ 4. Verbs whose stem ends in λ, μ, ν, or ρ are called two-termination verbs.

_____ 5. Rules of contraction should be applied when conjugating the present passive forms of the verb λύω.

_____ 6. There is no difference in meaning or emphasis between the second aorist form of the verb "we sinned" (ἡμάρτομεν) and the first aorist form of the verb "we sinned" (ἡμαρτήσαμεν).

_____ 7. The source of δηλοῖ is δηλάω.

_____ 8. The source of θεωρῶ is θεωρέω.

_____ 9. In theory, it is possible for both the rules of amalgamation and the rules of contraction to occur in the forming of a Greek verb whose stem ends in a vowel.

_____ 10. The liquid verb μένω contains a visible futuristic aspect morpheme in its future form.

GREEK to ENGLISH

Provide the English translation for each Greek sentence.

1. μαθητὴς σπείρει τὰ σπέρματα τῆς ἀληθείας ἐν ταῖς καρδίαις τοῦ λαοῦ τοῦ ἔθνους αὐτοῦ.

   _____

   _____

2. τὸ πνεῦμα τὸ ἅγιον παρακαλεῖ με ὅτι τὸ θέλημα τοῦ θεοῦ ἀγαθόν.

   _____

   _____

3. εὐχαριστοῦμεν τῷ θεῷ τῷ μόνῳ ὅτι πέμπει ἐλπίδα καὶ εἰρήνην τῷ λαῷ αὐτοῦ.

   _____

   _____

4. ὁ Μεσσίας τιμᾷ τὰς ἐντολὰς τοῦ πατρὸς αὐτοῦ καὶ βαπτίζει τοὺς ὄχλους κατὰ τὸ πνεῦμα τῆς ἀληθείας.

   _____

   _____

5. θέλουσιν οἱ λαοὶ βασιλέα, ἀλλ’ ἡ θέλημα τῶν λαῶν οὐκ ἔστιν ἡ θέλημα τοῦ θεοῦ.

   _____

   _____

6. ὁ ἀγαθὸς ἀνὴρ οἰκοδομήσει τὴν γυναῖκα αὐτοῦ παρὰ καλοῖς λόγοις.

   _____

   _____

7. ὁ ἱερεὺς ὁ ἀκάθαρτος οὐκ εὐλογεῖται ὑπὸ τῶν ὄχλων τῶν πιστῶν διὰ τὴν ἁμαρτίαν αὐτοῦ.

   _____

   _____

8. πλανᾷ καὶ ψεύδεται ὁ διάβολος καὶ τοῖς ἁμαρτωλοῖς καὶ τῷ σώματι τοῦ Χριστοῦ.

_____

_____

9. ὁ Ἰησοῦς ἐσταυρώθη ὑπὸ τῶν στρατιωτῶν, σήμερον δὲ αὐτὸς οὐκ ἔστιν νεκρός.

_____

_____

10. τὰ δαιμόνια τὰ κακὰ μισοῦσιν καὶ τοὺς λόγους καὶ τοὺς ἀγγέλους τοῦ θεοῦ.

_____

_____

11. ζητεῖς τὸ ὄνομα τοῦ κυρίου ἐν τῇ νυκτὶ ὅτι πιστεύεις ἐν τῇ ἐλπίδι τοῦ λόγου αὐτοῦ.

_____

_____

12. ὀψόμεθα τὴν σωτηρίαν τοῦ πατρὸς ἐν τῇ βασιλείᾳ καὶ οὐχὶ θεωρήσουσιν θάνατον.

_____

_____

13. ἐπληροῦντο οἱ ἀπόστολοὶ παρρησίᾳ ὑπὸ τοῦ ἁγίου πνεύματος, καὶ αὐτοὶ ἐκήρυσσον τὸν λόγον τοῦ θεοῦ τοῖς ὄχλοις.

_____

_____

14. καθ᾽ ἡμέραν ὁ ἁμαρτωλὸς οὐ προσκυνεῖ τὸν θεὸν τοῦ οὐρανοῦ καὶ γῆς.

_____

_____

15. δοκῶ ὅτι οἱ ἄνθρωποι πονηροὶ ἐν ταῖς καρδίαις αὐτῶν.

_____

_____

16. ὁ μάρτυς τοῦ εὐαγγελίου Χριστοῦ νικᾷ ἑκάστην θλῖψιν σὺν τῇ δυνάμει τοῦ θεοῦ.

_____

_____

17. ἡ μήτηρ δηλοῖ τὸν υἱὸν τὸν ἅγιον αὐτῆς ἐμοί, καὶ φέρω δῶρα αὐτῷ.

_____

_____

18. ἡ καρδία μου μαρτυρεῖ τῇ ἀληθείᾳ τῶν γραφῶν, καὶ κηρύσσω τοὺς λόγους τούτους τοῖς ὄχλοις.

_____

_____

19. ὁ διάκονος ὁ δίκαιος διακονεῖ ἐν τῷ ναῷ διὰ τὸν λόγον τοῦ κυρίου.

_____

_____

20. μεριμνᾷ ὁ δοῦλος περὶ τοῦ κυρίου αὐτοῦ καὶ τοῦ υἱοῦ τοῦ ἀγαθοῦ αὐτοῦ.

_____

_____

21. ὁ κύριος φιλεῖ τὰ παιδία αὐτοῦ, ἀλλ' ὁ ἐχθρὸς μισεῖ τὸν λαὸν τοῦ κόσμου τούτου.

_____

_____

22. τὰ ῥήματα τοῦ Χριστοῦ ἐρρέθησαν ὑπὸ τῶν ἀνδρῶν καὶ τῶν γυναικῶν τοῦ πνεύματος τοῦ ἁγίου.

_____

_____

23. δεθήσονται οἱ ἀπόστολοι ὑπὸ τοῦ ἀρχιερέως καὶ ἤρθησαν τῷ ναῷ ὑπὲρ τῆς κρίσεως αὐτῶν.

_____

_____

24. ζήσομαι ἐν Χριστῷ, καὶ οἱ τυφλοὶ λυθήσονται παρὰ τοῦ σκότους αὐτῶν.

    _____

    _____

25. ὁ μαθητὴς τετήρηκεν τὰς ἐντολὰς τῆς γραφῆς καὶ ἐν ταῖς ἐκκλησίαις καὶ τοῖς οἴκοις.

    _____

    _____

26. οἱ τελῶναι ἐκράτησαν δύναμιν καὶ ἐξουσίαν κατὰ τὰς πονηρὰς ἐπιθυμίας αὐτῶν.

    _____

    _____

27. τὰ δαιμόνια σκότους βλασφημοῦσιν τὸ ὄνομα τοῦ θεοῦ ἐν τοῖς οἴκοις τῆς ἁμαρτίας.

    _____

    _____

28. τὰ πλήθη ἐρωτᾷ τὸν Ἰησοῦν ὑπὲρ σημείου, οὐ δὲ ακούει τοὺς λόγους αὐτοῦ.

    _____

    _____

29. οἱ ἄρχοντες καὶ οἱ βασιλεῖς προσκυνοῦσιν τὸν πατέρα καὶ τὸν υἱὸν αὐτοῦ ἐν τῷ ναῷ τῆς προσευχῆς.

    _____

    _____

30. οἱ δοῦλοι τοῦ πατρὸς ἐκάλεσαν ἐπὶ τῶν ἰσχυρῶν νεανιῶν ὑπὲρ παρακλήσεως.

    _____

    _____

31. ὁ ἐχθρὸς ἀσθενεῖ ἐν τοῖς λόγοις αὐτοῦ, ὁ δὲ Ἰησοῦς ἐστιν ἰσχυρός.

    _____

    _____

32. οἱ ὑποκριταὶ τοῦ ναοῦ εὐλογοῦνται ὑπὸ τοῦ προφήτου διὰ τὴν σάρκα αὐτῶν καὶ τὴν ἁμαρτίαν αὐτῶν.

33. πεποιήκαμεν τὸ θέλημα τοῦ πατρὸς καὶ σωθησόμεθα ὑπ' αὐτοῦ.

34. ἐθεωροῦμεν ὅτι ὁ πονηρὸς ἄνθρωπος κακὸς ὅτι αὐτὸς οὐ φιλεῖ τὸν θεὸν ἡμῶν.

35. ὁ νεανίας ὁ δίκαιος αἰτεῖ τοὺς γραμματεῖς περὶ τῆς διδαχῆς τοῦ νόμου.

36. ἡ γυνὴ χάριτος γεννήσει ἐπὶ τῇ γῇ, ἀλλὰ τὸ παιδίον ἦν ὁ υἱὸς τοῦ θεοῦ ἀπ' οὐρανοῦ.

37. αἱ θυγατέρες τῆς ἀγάπης περιπατήσουσιν ἐν τῷ ὀνόματι τοῦ θεοῦ.

38. ἐζήτουν οἱ βασιλεῖς τῶν ἐθνῶν τὸ ἅγιον τέκνον ἐν τῇ νυκτί.

39. ὁ Ἰησοῦς πέμπει τοὺς μαθητάς, ἀλλ' οἱ ἀπόστολοι ἀκολουθοῦσιν αὐτὸν παρὰ τὴν θάλασσαν.

40. ὁ θεὸς τοῦ οὐρανοῦ ἠγάπησεν τὸν κόσμον καὶ ἔπεμψεν τὸν υἱὸν αὐτοῦ ὑπὲρ τῶν ἁμαρτιῶν ἡμῶν.

_____

_____

ENGLISH to GREEK

Provide the Greek translation for each English sentence.

1. The glory of God filled the temple and the throne of heaven.

    _____

    _____

2. The evil servant of death is weak, and he will not be healed.

    _____

    _____

3. The angels of heaven bless the Lord Jesus Christ with their mouths and their works.

    _____

    _____

4. The sinners of the darkness deceived the children with faithless wisdom.

    _____

    _____

5. Jesus called the disciples out of their boat and into His ministry.

    _____

    _____

6. The Holy Spirit sees the work of your (sg.) hands.

    _____

    _____

7.   The voice of an angel announces the gospel of Christ to the world.

_____

_____

8.   God took up the holy man to heaven, and he has the joy of the Lord.

_____

_____

9.   The gifts of the Spirit reveal the love, joy, and peace of Christ.

_____

_____

10.   The light of God has shown His love to His people.

_____

_____

20

PARTICIPLES (VERBAL ADJECTIVES)

Present Active Participles

GREEK to ENGLISH

Provide the English translation for each Greek sentence.

1. τὰ παιδία τὰ μανθάνοντα τὴν ἀληθείαν τῶν γραφῶν ἐδόξασεν καὶ τὸν θεὸν τοῦ οὐρανοῦ καὶ τὸ θέλημα τοῦ υἱοῦ αὐτοῦ.

2. ὁ ἀδελφὸς ὁ κηρύσσων τὸ εὐαγγέλιον τοῖς λαοῖς ἕξει καρδίαν ἀγάπης.

3. καταβαίνων ταύτῃ τῇ γῇ ὁ Ἰησοῦς εἶπεν λόγους εἰρήνης τοῖς μαθηταῖς.

4. ὁ πάσχων διὰ τὴν θλῖψιν τῆς σαρκὸς αὐτοῦ ἔπειθεν τὸν υἱὸν τοῦ θεοῦ.

5. αἱ διακονοῦσαι τοὺς διακόνους ἐν τῷ ναῷ ἑτοιμάζουσιν τὰς οἰκίας ὑπὲρ τῶν ἀνθρώπων τῶν λεγόντων αὐταῖς.

6. ἁμαρτάνουσα ἐν τῇ καρδίᾳ αὐτῆς ἡ θυγάτηρ τοῦ προφήτου οὐκ ἤκουσεν τοὺς λόγους τοῦ Χριστοῦ.

7. ὁ ἀπόστολος ὁ τιμῶν τὸν θεὸν τοῦ οὐρανοῦ ἄγει τοὺς ὄχλους ἐν δικαιοσύνῃ καὶ εἰρήνῃ.

_____

_____

ENGLISH to GREEK

Provide the Greek translation for each English sentence.

1. The church heals those men who are suffering from their sins.

   _____

   _____

2. I wrote a letter to the man who was preparing the way of the Lord.

   _____

   _____

3. Jesus, who was speaking against the devil and his demons, was casting them out of the unclean man.

   _____

   _____

4. While teaching the crowds about the grace of God, she sees the Messiah.

   _____

   _____

5. The children that are saying these things are being healed by God.

   _____

   _____

6. This woman is not the one who is hearing the voice of God.

   _____

   _____

7. While he is in the temple, he glorifies God.

_____

_____

Present Middle and Passive Participles

GREEK to ENGLISH

Provide the English translation for each Greek sentence.

1. οἱ ἀδελφοὶ οἱ τηρούμενοι τῇ ὁδῷ τῆς δικαιοσύνης ὑπὸ τοῦ κυρίου ἐδόξασαν τὸν ἀμνὸν τοῦ θεοῦ.

_____

_____

2. ἡ λεγομένη ταῦτα κηρύσσει περὶ τῶν πονηρῶν προφητῶν ἐν τῷ κόσμῳ.

_____

_____

3. βαπτιζόμενος ὑπὸ τοῦ προφήτου τοῦ καινοῦ ἐν τῇ θαλάσσῃ ἐγὼ γίνομαι τέκνον θεοῦ.

_____

_____

4. ὁ ἀνὴρ ὁ ζητούμενος ὑπὸ τοῦ ἐλέους τοῦ Χριστοῦ ἀγαπᾷ τοὺς ἀδελφοὺς αὐτοῦ καὶ τὸν θεὸν αὐτοῦ.

_____

_____

5. οἱ φανερούμενοι τὰς ἀληθείας ἐν ταῖς γραφαῖς ἔπεισαν τὴν δύναμιν τοῦ ἁγίου πνεύματος.

_____

_____

6. ἀποστελλόμενος εἰς τὴν ἐκκλησίαν ὑπὸ τοῦ ἀνδρὸς τοῦ θεοῦ ὁ κακὸς νεανίας μισεῖται ὑπὸ τῶν υἱῶν καὶ θυγατέρων τοῦ θεοῦ.

_____

_____

7. τὰ δῶρα τοῦ κυρίου τὰ φερόμενα τοῖς παιδίοις ὑπὸ τοῦ πατρὸς αὐτῶν ἐλήμφθησαν μετὰ χαρᾶς.

_____

_____

ENGLISH to GREEK

Provide the Greek translation for each English sentence.

1. The nations that are being healed by the Lord are praying to God.

_____

_____

2. While being baptized by the apostle, the small man sees the glory of God.

_____

_____

3. The hypocrite who was being seen by the devil was leading the people who were being taught evil things.

_____

_____

4. The grace of God that will be seen in the world will glorify God.

_____

_____

5. The truth of Christ is preparing the young men who are teaching themselves the truths of Christ.

_____

_____

6. While being seen by the eyes of the Lord, the prophet preached the gospel to the women who were hearing it for themselves.

_____

_____

7. The children who are learning the truths of Christ for themselves love the Lord.

_____

_____

First Aorist Active Participles

GREEK to ENGLISH

Provide the English translation for each Greek sentence.

1. τὰ τέκνα τὰ ἀκούσαντα τὴν διδαχὴν Χριστοῦ ἐστιν ἀγαθά.

_____

_____

2. οἱ πείσαντες τὸν κύριον ἐν ταῖς καρδίαις αὐτῶν ἐδόξασαν τὸν υἱὸν τοῦ θεοῦ ἐν τῷ ναῷ.

_____

_____

3. λύσας τοὺς δούλους παρὰ τοῦ σκότους ἐκήρυσσεν τὸ εὐαγγέλιον ἐν τῷ νεκρῷ κόσμῳ.

_____

_____

4. εὐλογήσαντες τοὺς πιστοὺς λήμψεσθε δύναμιν ἀπὸ τοῦ ἁγίου πνεύματος.

_____

_____

5. ὁ γράψας τὸ βιβλίον ἐν τῷ οἴκῳ αὐτοῦ ἠγέρθη ὑπὸ τοῦ κυρίου κατὰ τὸ θέλημα τοῦ θεοῦ.

_____

_____

6. ὁ λύσας τὰς κακὰς ἀπὸ τῶν ἁμαρτιῶν αὐτῶν ἐστιν ὁ σώσας τοὺς κακοὺς ἐν τῷ ἱερῷ.

_____

_____

7. ὁ ἀνὴρ ὁ ἑτοιμάσας τὴν καρδίαν αὐτοῦ ὑπὲρ τοῦ Χριστοῦ ἀγαπᾷ τὸν λόγον τοῦ θεοῦ.

_____

_____

ENGLISH to GREEK

Provide the Greek translation for each English sentence.

1. I know the Christ who saw me from the cross.

_____

_____

2. Christ died for the world that had not believed in Him.

_____

_____

3. The prophet came to the same crowds who had not trusted in the Messiah.

_____

_____

4. Christ opens the kingdom of heaven to those men who believed in Him.

_____

_____

5. The love of God is being written upon the hearts of the men who heard the truths of Christ.

_____

_____

6. I send the servants to the children who heard the truth.

_____

_____

7. The faithful children were loosing themselves from the ones who had taught them evil things.

_____

_____

First Aorist Middle Participles

GREEK to ENGLISH

Provide the English translation for each Greek sentence.

1. ὁ προφήτης ὁ εὑράμενος τὰ ἀγαπητὰ τέκνα τοῦ θεοῦ καλεῖ τὸν λαὸν ταῖς ἐντολαῖς τοῦ θεοῦ.

_____

_____

2. ἡ δεξαμένη τὰ ῥήματα τοῦ ἀποστόλου διδάξει τοὺς ὄχλους περὶ τῶν γραφῶν καὶ τῆς ἀληθείας τοῦ Χριστοῦ.

_____

_____

3. ἐργασάμενος ἐν τῷ κόσμῳ Ἰησοῦς Χριστὸς ἐκήρυξεν περὶ τῆς κρίσεως κατὰ τὸ θέλημα τοῦ πατρὸς αὐτοῦ ἐν οὐρανῷ.

_____

_____

4. τὰ ἔθνη τὰ γενόμενα δοῦλοι οὐ προσεύχεται τῷ θεῷ.

5. προσευξάμενοι ὑπὲρ τῆς σωτηρίας αὐτῶν ἔλαβον αἰώνιον θάνατον διὰ τὴν ἁμαρτίαν αὐτῶν.

6. εὑρέθημεν ὑπὸ τῶν εὐαγγελισαμένων ἡμῖν περὶ τῶν ἁμαρτιῶν ἡμῶν.

7. λογισάμενον ὑπὲρ τὸ ὄνομα Χριστοῦ τὸ τέκνον τοῦ διαβόλου οὐκ ἐκήρυξεν τὰς ἀληθείας Χριστοῦ τοῖς ὄχλοις.

ENGLISH to GREEK

Provide the Greek translation for each English sentence.

1. After they taught themselves the truths of Christ, the strong women will hear another word of the Lord.

2. I know the Christ who did not loose himself from the cross.

3. After they themselves had glorified the Son, the men glorified the Father.

4. After he had loosed himself, the apostle went to Peter's house.

5. Having healed themselves from their affliction, the people glorify God.

6. The servant of the Lord receives the one who taught herself the holy Scriptures.

7. Having seen themselves through the eyes of a holy God, the people call upon the name of the Lord.

First and Second Aorist Passive Participles

GREEK to ENGLISH

Provide the English translation for each Greek sentence.

1. ὁ μάρτυς ὁ εὑρεθεὶς σοφὸς ὑπὸ τῶν ἀγγέλων ἔφυγεν εἰς τὴν ἔρημον.

2. τὰ ῥήματα περὶ τῆς ζωῆς Χριστοῦ τὰ γραφέντα ἐν ταῖς ἁγίαις γραφαῖς ἐστιν οἱ λόγοι τοῦ θεοῦ.

3. βαπτισθὲν ὑπὸ τοῦ ἁγίου πνεύματος τὸ πλῆθος προσκυνεῖ τὸν κύριον παρ' ἁγίαις φωναῖς.

4. οἱ δοῦλοι οἱ λυθέντες παρὰ τῶν ἁμαρτιῶν αὐτῶν ἐλήμφθησαν εἰς τὴν βασιλείαν τοῦ θεοῦ ὑπὸ τοῦ πατρός.

_____

_____

5. οἱ σωθέντες διὰ τῆς δυνάμεως τοῦ λόγου αὐτοῦ ἐδόξαζον τὸν μόνον θεόν.

_____

_____

6. τελειωθεὶς ὑπὸ τοῦ ἔργου τῆς διακονίας ὁ ἀπόστολος λαλεῖ τὴν ἀλήθειαν τοῖς ὄχλοις ἐν τῇ συναγωγῇ.

_____

_____

7. ὁ Χριστὸς ὁ δοξασθεὶς ὑπὸ τοῦ πατρὸς αὐτοῦ οὐκ ἁμαρτάνει ἐν τῇ σαρκὶ αὐτοῦ.

_____

_____

ENGLISH to GREEK

Provide the Greek translation for each English sentence.

1. I am a servant of the master who loosed me.

_____

_____

2. I received the gift of eternal life from the Lord, who healed me from my sins.

_____

_____

3. Having been healed from a life of sin, the child fled from the evil temple.

_____

_____

4. The truths of Christ that have been written in the book of life will lead a man to eternal life.

_____

_____

5. The blind man who was left in the temple by his friends is not a wise man.

_____

_____

6. The child saw the writings that had been written by the apostle himself.

_____

_____

7. The man who had been baptized by the strong woman went into the house.

_____

_____

Second Aorist Active Participles

GREEK to ENGLISH

Provide the English translation for each Greek sentence.

1. τὰ μικρὰ παιδία τὰ λαβόντα σωτηρίαν ἀπὸ τοῦ κυρίου τιμᾷ τὸν πατέρα τοῦ οὐρανοῦ καὶ γῆς.

_____

_____

2. ὁ γνοὺς τὰς ἁγίας γραφὰς παρὰ τοῦ πρώτου ἔτους ἐκήρυξεν τὸ εὐαγγέλιον.

_____

_____

3. μαθόντες περὶ τοῦ αἵματος τοῦ Χριστοῦ οἱ υἱοὶ ἔλαβον τὸ πνεῦμα ἐν ταῖς καρδίαις αὐτῶν.

_____

_____

4. οἱ ἄγγελοι οἱ ἐκβαλόντες τὰ δαιμόνια ἐκ οὐρανοῦ οὐκ ἔρχονται τῇ γῇ σὺν αὐτοῖς.

_____

_____

5. ἡ λαβοῦσα ἄρτον ἀπὸ τοῦ ναοῦ οὐκ ἔπεισεν τὴν χάριτα τοῦ θεοῦ.

_____

_____

6. εὑρόντα τὰ δῶρα ἐν τῷ ἱερῷ τὰ τέκνα τῶν τελωνῶν ἐδόξαζεν θεόν.

_____

_____

7. ὁ δοῦλος ὁ φαγὼν τὸν ἄρτον ἐν τῇ ἐρήμῳ ἐθεραπεύθη ὑπὸ τοῦ θεοῦ αὐτοῦ.

_____

_____

ENGLISH to GREEK

Provide the Greek translation for each English sentence.

1. God honors the one who saw the sin of man.

_____

_____

2. The strong child who learned about the grace of God is being loosed by the Lord.

_____

_____

3. The church that had learned about the evil sayings has healed the hearts of its people.

_____

_____

4. Having left the glory of heaven, Christ will glorify His Father in heaven.

---

5. Jesus, who had spoken against the devil and his demons, was casting them out of the unclean man.

---

6. Jesus taught that He was the one who had suffered for all men.

---

7. God loves the good woman who learned about the way of salvation.

Second Aorist Middle Participles

GREEK to ENGLISH

Provide the English translation for each Greek sentence.

1. ὁ προφήτης ὁ εὑράμενος θεὸν καλεῖ πρὸς θεὸν ἐν ἑτέρᾳ γλώσσῃ.

---

2. ὁ λαβόμενος τὴν θυγατέρα αὐτοῦ πρὸς τὸ ὕδωρ καὶ ἐβαπτίσατο αὐτήν.

---

3. ὁ γενόμενος καλὸς ἄνθρωπος καὶ ἐδικαιώθη ὑπὸ τοῦ θανάτου Ἰησοῦ.

---

4. μεταβαλόμενοι (from μεταβάλλω, meaning "to change one's mind about") τὴν ἀλήθειαν τοῦ Χριστοῦ ἦλθον ἐκ τῆς συναγωγῆς καὶ εἰς τὸν οἶκον.

   _____

   _____

5. ἔδοξεν ἡμῖν γενομένοις ἄρχουσιν τῆς συναγωγῆς ὅτι κακοὶ ἄνθρωποι ἐδικαιώθησαν ὑπὸ πίστεως καθὼς καλοὶ ἄνθρωποι ἐδικαιώθησαν ὑπὸ πίστεως.

   _____

   _____

6. ἀπεκτάνθησαν ὑπὸ τοῦ διαγενομένου (from διαγίνομαι, meaning "to go through, to pass") τὸ ἱερὸν τὸ πονηρόν.

   _____

   _____

7. ἐπιλαβόμενος (from ἐπιλαμβάνομαι, meaning "to take hold of") ἐν τῷ φωτὶ τοῦ ἀληθείας τοῦ θεοῦ ὁ ἀνὴρ ἔλαβεν σωτηρίαν ἀπὸ τοῦ κυρίου.

   _____

   _____

ENGLISH to GREEK

Provide the Greek translation for each English sentence.

1. Having left themselves in the synagogue, the strong women did not hear the voice of God.

   _____

   _____

2. I honor the Christ who did not leave Himself in the world.

   _____

   _____

3. After they themselves had left the church, the men were reading the good book.

   _____

   _____

4. After he had seen himself in the light, the disciple had fear in his heart.

_____

_____

5. Having learned for themselves the truths of God, the people will show their love to Him.

_____

_____

6. The man considers the one who learned for herself the holy Scriptures.

_____

_____

7. Having seen themselves through the eyes of a holy God, the people call upon the name of the Lord.

_____

_____

Perfect Active Participles

GREEK to ENGLISH

Provide the English translation for each Greek sentence.

1. κεκληκὼς τὸν δοῦλον ἀπὸ τοῦ οἴκου αὐτοῦ τὸ τέκνον λαμβάνει αἰώνιον ζωήν.

_____

_____

2. ὁ ἡμαρτηκὼς ἔβαλεν τὸν πονηρὸν προφήτην ἐκ τοῦ ἱεροῦ τοῦ θεοῦ.

_____

_____

3. ἐγνωκότες περὶ τῆς δικαιοσύνης Χριστοῦ ἔτι οἱ ἄπιστοι οὐκ ἐδόξασαν τὸν θεόν.

_____

_____

4. εἰδὼς τὸν νόμον τοῦ θεοῦ ἐπὶ ταῖς καρδίαις τῶν ἀνθρώπων ὁ θεὸς εὐλογεῖ τὰ τέκνα αὐτοῦ.

   _____

   _____

5. ἐγὼ εἶπον ὅτι τιμᾷ τὸν πεπονθότα Χριστὸν ὑπὲρ τῶν ἁμαρτιῶν αὐτῶν.

   _____

   _____

6. οὐ πέποιθα τὸν μὴ πεφευγότα ἀπὸ τῆς ἁμαρτίας αὐτοῦ καὶ τῆς σαρκὸς αὐτοῦ.

   _____

   _____

7. ἐγὼ οὐχ ἑτοιμάσω τὸν οἶκόν μου ὑπὲρ τοῦ πονηροῦ κυρίου τοῦ μὴ εἰδότος τὸν δοῦλον αὐτοῦ.

   _____

   _____

ENGLISH to GREEK

Provide the Greek translation for each English sentence.

1. The women who have loosed the servants are good women.

   _____

   _____

2. Having found the Lord, the brother remains in the temple.

   _____

   _____

3. I will not trust in the evil apostle who has not trusted in Christ.

   _____

   _____

4. Were you casting the woman, who had thrown the good apostles out of the temple, out of the house?

    _____

    _____

5. Daily I come to the temple and pray to the one who has loosed me from my sins.

    _____

    _____

6. We came to the place that had healed me.

    _____

    _____

7. The one who has suffered many things for us is the Holy One of God.

    _____

    _____

Perfect Middle and Passive Participles

GREEK to ENGLISH

Provide the English translation for each Greek sentence.

1. λελυμένον ὑπὸ τοῦ πατρὸς αὐτοῦ τὸ παιδίον τιμᾷ τὸν πατέρα αὐτοῦ.

    _____

    _____

2. ὁ υἱὸς τοῦ θεοῦ ἡτοίμακεν τὴν ὁδὸν ὑπὲρ τῶν τέκνων τῶν λελυμένων τῷ λόγῳ τοῦ θεοῦ.

    _____

    _____

3. τεθεραπευμέναι ὑπὸ τοῦ ἀποστόλου τοῦ ἀγαθοῦ αἱ γυναῖκες ἐκήρυξαν περὶ τῆς ἀγάπης τοῦ θεοῦ.

_____

_____

4. ὁ αὐτὸς κύριος ζητεῖ καὶ σῴζει τὰ πεπιστευμένα.

_____

_____

5. ἐκβεβλημένη ἐκ τοῦ οἴκου ὑπὸ πονηροῦ προφήτου ἡ αὐτὴ θυγάτηρ εἶδεν τὸν κύριον σὺν τοῖς ὀφθαλμοῖς αὐτῆς.

_____

_____

6. λελυμένοι ἀπὸ τῶν ἁμαρτιῶν ἡμῶν ἐσόμεθα τὰ τέκνα τοῦ θεοῦ.

_____

_____

7. λέγουσιν ὅτι ὁ Ἰησοῦς οὐκ ἔσωσεν ἡμᾶς, ἀλλ᾽ αὐτοί ἐσμεν οἱ σεσωσμένοι ἀπὸ τῶν ἁμαρτιῶν ἡμῶν.

_____

_____

ENGLISH to GREEK

Provide the Greek translation for each English sentence.

1. Having been thrown out of the temple, the evil children went into the house.

_____

_____

2. I am the man who has been saved from my sins.

_____

_____

3. The same man who has been healed by the Lord is the same man who has believed for himself the truths of Christ.

_____

_____

4. You are the women who have been saved by the Holy Spirit.

_____

_____

5. You (pl.) will be a child of God who has been healed by the Holy One.

_____

_____

6. The Lord blesses me because I preach about the One who has loosed me from my sins.

_____

_____

7. We love the Lord with hearts that have been loosed by Him.

_____

_____

Periphrastic Participles

GREEK to ENGLISH

Provide the English translation for each Greek sentence.

1. ἐγώ εἰμι λύων τοὺς δούλους, ἀλλὰ σὺ εἶ βλέπων τοὺς ὄχλους.

_____

_____

2. σὺ εἶ σῴζων ἀφ' ἁμαρτίας, ἀλλ' ἐγώ εἰμι σῳζόμενος.

_____

_____

3. χάριτι γάρ ἐστε σεσωσμένοι διὰ πίστεως.

_____

_____

4. εἰμὶ οὖν ζῶν κατὰ τὴν ἀλήθειαν ὅτι γέγραπται ὑπὸ θεοῦ ὑπὲρ μοῦ.

_____

_____

5. εἰ προσευχόμενος προσευχὴν τῷ θεῷ ἀλλ' οὐκ ἔσῃ ἀκούων τὴν φωνὴν τοῦ θεοῦ ἐν τῷ ἱερῷ.

_____

_____

6. ὁ ἀνὴρ ἦν ψευδόμενος τοῖς ἁγίοις ἀποστόλοις.

_____

_____

7. ἧς ὁρῶν ταῦτα, εἰ ὁρῶσα ταῦτα, καὶ ἔσῃ ποιοῦν ταῦτα.

_____

_____

ENGLISH to GREEK

Provide the Greek translation for each English sentence.

1. He was sending the evil prophet into the synagogues, but I was receiving a word from the Lord.

_____

_____

2. Paul was hearing a voice from God on the road to the synagogue.

_____

_____

3. The gods of this earth are not saving the men from their sins.

    _____

    _____

4. I was coming toward the house, but you were not going into it.

    _____

    _____

5. I am learning about the truths of Christ.

    _____

    _____

6. I (masc./sg.) was reading the holy Scriptures in the temple, but you (fem./ sg.) were eating around the sea.

    _____

    _____

7. I am praying to God in a different language.

    _____

    _____

Genitive Absolute

GREEK to ENGLISH

Provide the English translation for each Greek sentence.

1. τελειωσάντων τοὺς πιστούς, λήμψονται δύναμιν ἀπὸ τοῦ ἁγίου πνεύματος.

    _____

    _____

2. ἁμαρτούσης τῆς μητρὸς κατὰ θεοῦ, ἡ εκκλησία ἐδίδαξεν τὰς ἀληθείας τοῦ θεοῦ ἀπὸ τοῦ καλοῦ βιβλίου.

    _____

3. εἰπόντων τῶν μαθητῶν, οἱ ἀπόστολοι οἱ ἅγιοι ἐκήρυξαν κατὰ τῶν ἁμαρτιῶν αὐτῶν.

_____

_____

4. ἐξερχομένων τῶν μαθητῶν ἐκ τοῦ ἱεροῦ, οἱ ἀγαθοὶ θεραπεύουσιν τὸν λαόν.

_____

_____

5. ἀκουσάντων ταῦτα, λήμψονται τὸ ἅγιον πνεῦμα.

_____

_____

6. παθόντος εἰς τὴν σάρκα, ὁ ἰσχυρὸς ζητήσει τὸν κύριον ἐν τῷ ἱερῷ.

_____

_____

7. βεβληκότος τὸν δοῦλον εἰς τὴν ἔρημον, αὐτὴ ἔπεμψεν αὐτὸν εἰς τὴν ἐκκλησίαν.

_____

_____

ENGLISH to GREEK

Provide the Greek translation for each English sentence.

1. After they had left the servant, the apostle preached about the love of God.

_____

_____

2. While the world did not believe in Him, Christ died on the cross.

_____

_____

3. While the apostle is teaching the holy Scriptures, the disciple asks the good man about the truths of Christ.

_____

_____

4. After the disciples were saying these things, the good women glorified God.

_____

_____

5. While he was God, the apostle did not believe in Him.

_____

_____

6. After they had been loosed by the Lord, the servant heard the voice of the Lord.

_____

_____

7. While she was hearing from the Lord, the peace of God was being seen upon the earth.

_____

_____

All Participial Forms

GREEK to ENGLISH

Provide the English translation for each Greek sentence.

1. ἡ ζητοῦσα τὴν ζωὴν τὴν αἰώνιον πιστεύει ἐν τῇ ἀναστάσει τοῦ Χριστοῦ.

_____

_____

2. οἱ δικαιωθέντες εἰς τὴν ἐκκλησίαν ὑπὸ τοῦ αἵματος τοῦ Χριστοῦ ἔπασχον τὴν ὀργὴν τοῦ ἐχθροῦ.

_____

_____

3. ὁ σώσας τὸν τυφλὸν ἀπὸ τοῦ σκότους αὐτοῦ εἶπεν περὶ τῆς δόξης τοῦ ἁγίου.

4. ὁ μὴ καλούμενος ὑπὸ τῶν ὄχλων ἦν ὁ κύριος ὑπὲρ πάντων.

5. ὁ θεὸς ἐδοξάσθη ὑπὸ τοῦ παθόντος θλῖψιν ἐπὶ τῇ γῇ.

6. καλοῦντος τοῦ τέκνου, ὁ ἄνθρωπος ἔλιπεν τὴν ἐκκλησίαν αὐτοῦ.

7. ὁ υἱὸς τοῦ θεοῦ ἐστιν φέρων εἰρήνην, ἀλλ᾽ οὐκ ἔσεσθε πιστεύοντες εἰς αὐτόν.

8. οὐκ ἐπιστεύθη ὅτι ὁ κύριος ζητήσει τοὺς ἀνθρώπους τοὺς μὴ σεσωσμένους διὰ τοῦ ἁγίου πνεύματος.

9. θεωρῶ ὅτι εἶ ὁ ἄνθρωπος ὁ καλούμενος εἰς τὸ φῶς.

10. θεωρήσαντες τὰς ἁγίας γραφάς, οἱ ἄνθρωποι προσκυνοῦσιν τὸν πατέρα ἐν οὐρανῷ.

11. φεύγων εἰς τὴν ἔρημον, ὁ προφήτης προσηύχετο τῷ πατρὶ αὐτοῦ ἐν οὐρανῷ.

_____

_____

12. καλούμενος ὑπὸ τοῦ ἁγίου πνεύματος, ὁ ἀπόστολος εὐχαριστεῖ ὑπὲρ τῆς χαρᾶς τῆς σωτηρίας αὐτοῦ.

_____

_____

13. ἀκούσας τὸ εὐαγγέλιον ἐν ἑτέρᾳ γλώσσῃ, ὁ βασιλεὺς ἐκβάλλει τοὺς ἀποστόλους ἐκ τῶν ἐκκλησιῶν.

_____

_____

14. πεμφθέντες εἰς τὸν κόσμον, οἱ ἀδελφοὶ λύουσιν τοὺς στρατιώτας ἀπὸ τοῦ θλίψεως αὐτῶν.

_____

_____

15. ἀκουόμενοι ὑπὸ τοῦ κυρίου, οἱ κακοὶ ἄνθρωποι σωθήσονται ὑπὸ τοῦ ἁγίου τέκνου.

_____

_____

16. τὸ αἷμα τοῦ Χριστοῦ τὸ ἑτοιμάζον τὴν ὁδὸν τοῦ κυρίου οὐ λαμβάνεται ὑπὸ τοῦ ἀπίστων ὑποκριτῶν.

_____

_____

17. πεπεισμένοι τὰς καλὰς ἀληθείας Χριστοῦ, οἱ πατέρες δοξάσουσιν τὸ ὄνομα τοῦ κυρίου.

_____

_____

18. ἀγαπᾷς τοὺς τηρήσαντας σε ἀπὸ τῶν ἁμαρτιῶν σου.

_____

_____

19. βεβλημένη ἐκ τοῦ ἱεροῦ ὑπὸ τοῦ ἱερέως, ἡ θυγάτηρ ἐπίστευσεν εἰς Χριστόν.

_____

_____

20. οἱ ἄπιστοι ἦσαν βλασφημοῦντες τὸν ἅγιον υἱὸν τοῦ θεοῦ.

_____

_____

21. λεγόντων τῶν ἀποστόλων ταῦτα, οἱ μαθηταὶ ἐξῆλθον ἐκ τοῦ οἴκου.

_____

_____

22. μαρτυροῦντος τοῦ ἄρχοντος πρὸς τὸν δοῦλον, ὁ ἕτερος ἄρχων ἔβλεψεν τοὺς ὄχλους.

_____

_____

23. ὁ ἅγιος ἄνθρωπος τοῦ θεοῦ ὁ φέρων τὰς ἁμαρτίας ἡμῶν ἐδίδαξεν τὸ θέλημα τοῦ πατρὸς ἡμῶν.

_____

_____

24. οἱ ἐχθροὶ τῆς ὁδοῦ οἱ φανερούμενοι τῷ ὄχλῳ βλασφημοῦσιν τὸ ὄνομα τοῦ Χριστοῦ.

_____

_____

25. αἱ προσευχαὶ αἱ ἐξελθοῦσαι ἐκ τῶν καρδιῶν τῶν ἁμαρτωλῶν τιμῶσιν τὸ ἰσχυρὸν ἔργον τοῦ θεοῦ.

_____

_____

26. προσευξάμενος πρὸς τὸν πονηρὸν θεόν, ὁ ἀρχιερεὺς ἐπίστευσεν ἐν τῷ υἱῷ τοῦ θεοῦ.

_____

_____

27. τὰ ῥήματα τοῦ βασιλέως τὰ ἀποστελλόμενα ὑπὸ τοῦ δούλου οὐκ ἐλήμφθη διὰ τοῦ ἀρχιερέως.

_____

_____

28. εἰπὼν ταῦτα, τὸ πονηρὸν τέκνον οὐκ εἶπεν λόγους θανάτου.

_____

_____

29. βληθεὶς ἐκ τοῦ ναοῦ, ὁ δοῦλος ἐσθίει ἄρτον καὶ καρπόν.

_____

_____

30. ψεύδῃ ὅτε σὺ λέγει ὅτι ἦς ὁ ἑτοιμάσας τὴν ὁδὸν τοῦ κυρίου.

_____

_____

31. πεπιστευκότες τὸν λόγον τῆς ἀληθείας, οἱ μάρτυρες ἦλθον εἰς τὴν ἐκκλησίαν τοῦ θεοῦ.

_____

_____

32. ἐγώ εἰμι δεδικαιωμένος ἀπὸ τῆς ἁμαρτίας μου, ἀλλ᾽ ὑμεῖς οὐκ ἐστὲ τεθεραπευμέναι ἀπὸ τῶν ἁμαρτιῶν ὑμῶν.

_____

_____

33. ἡ χάρις τοῦ θεοῦ ἡ φέρουσα σωτηρίαν οὐ λημφθήσεται ὑπὸ πάντων τῶν ἀνθρώπων.

_____

_____

34. ὁ ἄρχων ἐν τῇ συναγωγῇ ἐστιν ἀγαθὸς ἄρχων.

_____

_____

35. φιλῶ τοὺς φίλους μου, ἀλλ᾽ ἀγαπῶ τὸν λαμβανόμενόν με εἰς τὴν βασιλείαν αὐτοῦ.

_____

_____

36. ὁ προφήτης ἐστὶν κηρύσσων κατὰ τῆς ἁμαρτίας μου καὶ τῆς πονηρᾶς σαρκός μου, ἀλλ᾽ οὐκ ἀκήκοα λόγους ἀγάπης ἀπ᾽ αὐτοῦ.

_____

_____

All Participial Forms

ENGLISH to GREEK

Provide the Greek translation for each English sentence.

1. While reading the holy Scriptures, I ask the good disciple about the truths of Christ.

   _____

   _____

2. After the Holy Spirit comes upon you, you will receive power.

   _____

   _____

3. We were preparing the way of the Lord, but you (pl.) are not trusting in the truth.

   _____

   _____

4. Having believed for himself the truths in the good book, the man preached about the Son of God.

   _____

   _____

5. The things that are being taught by the apostles are not good things.

    _____

    _____

6. After they had prepared themselves for the way of the Lord, the disciples spoke about the glory of God.

    _____

    _____

7. The teachings of Christ that were taught to the crowds are not evil.

    _____

    _____

8. The women who sent the gifts to the friends of the dead soldiers are good.

    _____

    _____

9. Does the church receive grace and mercy from the one who left the glory of heaven?

    _____

    _____

10. After they themselves had suffered for the name of the Lord, the disciples spoke about the glory of God.

    _____

    _____

11. No one believes that the devil, who has learned the Scriptures, is a good person.

    _____

    _____

12. Will you (sg.) be healing the unclean women today?

    _____

    _____

13. The God of heaven and earth will heal these men who will be loosing the servants.

_____

_____

14. The devil sees the men who are not being saved by the Lord.

_____

_____

15. The gift that sent peace into the world is not being received.

_____

_____

16. The good woman brings gifts to the good slaves who loosed themselves from their bad masters.

_____

_____

17. After He was left by his mother and father, Jesus taught the people in the temple.

_____

_____

18. Having seen the Lord, the wise men will glorify God.

_____

_____

19. The good man brings bad gifts to the new slaves who threw themselves out of their masters' houses.

_____

_____

20. Having saved His people from their sins, the Lord preached about the joy of the Lord.

_____

_____

21. You (masc. pl.), who have been saved by the grace of God, will glorify the God of grace and peace.

_____

_____

22. After they spoke to themselves in the flesh, the men preached against their sin.

_____

_____

23. The cross of Christ received glory from the children who were preaching about His love.

_____

_____

24. God loves you, but He does not love the sin that is proclaiming itself against Him.

_____

_____

25. The fear of the Lord does not bring peace to the man who did not believe in the Messiah.

_____

_____

26. I am a woman who taught herself about the teachings of Christ.

_____

_____

27. Having been taught these things, the chief priest loves the Lord.

_____

_____

28.   The strong women who spoke these truths are beautiful women.

_____

_____

29.   I am a woman who learned for herself the teachings of Christ.

_____

_____

30.   I have not loosed the children who had found the Lord.

_____

_____

31.   God, who has loosed for Himself His children, is a good God.

_____

_____

32.   You will be loosing the servants from the evil temple.

_____

_____

33.   After they taught themselves the holy Scriptures, the apostles heard from the Lord.

_____

_____

34.   Jesus will be glorified after the crowd sees a sign from Him.

_____

_____

35.   My faith is not being seen by the disciples, but it is being seen by God.

_____

_____

21

INFINITIVES (VERBAL NOUNS)

GREEK to ENGLISH

Provide the English translation for each Scripture.

1. λέγει αὐτῷ Ναθαναήλ· πόθεν με γινώσκεις; ἀπεκρίθη Ἰησοῦς καὶ εἶπεν αὐτῷ· πρὸ τοῦ σε Φίλιππον φωνῆσαι ὄντα ὑπὸ τὴν συκῆν εἶδόν σε.

   _____

   _____

2. καὶ διὰ τὸ ὁμότεχνον εἶναι ἔμενεν παρ’ αὐτοῖς, καὶ ἠργάζετο· ἦσαν γὰρ σκηνοποιοὶ τῇ τέχνῃ.

   _____

   _____

3. τοὺς γὰρ πάντας ἡμᾶς φανερωθῆναι δεῖ ἔμπροσθεν τοῦ βήματος τοῦ Χριστοῦ, ἵνα κομίσηται ἕκαστος τὰ διὰ τοῦ σώματος πρὸς ἃ ἔπραξεν, εἴτε ἀγαθὸν εἴτε φαῦλον.

   _____

   _____

4. πάντοτε μανθάνοντα καὶ μηδέποτε εἰς ἐπίγνωσιν ἀληθείας ἐλθεῖν δυνάμενα.

   _____

   _____

5. δι’ ἣν αἰτίαν οὐκ ἐπαισχύνεται ἀδελφοὺς αὐτοὺς καλεῖν.

   _____

   _____

6. ὁ λέγων ἐν αὐτῷ μένειν ὀφείλει καθὼς ἐκεῖνος περιεπάτησεν καὶ αὐτὸς [οὕτως] περιπατεῖν.

   _____

   _____

7. ὃς γὰρ ἐὰν θέλῃ τὴν ψυχὴν αὐτοῦ σῶσαι ἀπολέσει αὐτήν· ὃς δ' ἂν ἀπολέσῃ τὴν ψυχὴν αὐτοῦ ἕνεκεν ἐμοῦ εὑρήσει αὐτήν.

---

8. καὶ θέλων αὐτὸν ἀποκτεῖναι ἐφοβήθη (he feared) τὸν ὄχλον, ὅτι ὡς προφήτην αὐτὸν εἶχον.

---

9. πνεῦμα κυρίου ἐπ' ἐμὲ οὗ εἵνεκεν ἔχρισέν με εὐαγγελίσασθαι πτωχοῖς, ἀπέσταλκέν με, κηρύξαι αἰχμαλώτοις ἄφεσιν καὶ τυφλοῖς ἀνάβλεψιν, ἀποστεῖλαι τεθραυσμένους ἐν ἀφέσει.

---

10. οἱ πατέρες ἡμῶν ἐν τῷ ὄρει τούτῳ προσεκύνησαν· καὶ ὑμεῖς λέγετε ὅτι ἐν Ἱεροσολύμοις ἐστὶν ὁ τόπος ὅπου προσκυνεῖν δεῖ.

---

11. Ἐν δὲ τῷ πορεύεσθαι ἐγένετο αὐτὸν ἐγγίζειν τῇ Δαμασκῷ, ἐξαίφνης τε αὐτὸν περιήστραψεν φῶς ἐκ τοῦ οὐρανοῦ.

---

12. Βλέπετε οὖν πῶς ἀκούετε· ὃς ἂν γὰρ ἔχῃ, δοθήσεται αὐτῷ· καὶ ὃς ἂν μὴ ἔχῃ, καὶ ὃ δοκεῖ ἔχειν ἀρθήσεται ἀπ' αὐτοῦ.

---

13. Καὶ ἐγένετο αὐτὸν ἐν τοῖς σάββασιν παραπορεύεσθαι διὰ τῶν σπορίμων, καὶ οἱ μαθηταὶ αὐτοῦ ἤρξαντο ὁδὸν ποιεῖν τίλλοντες τοὺς στάχυας.

---

14. ἐν δὲ τῷ ἄρξασθαί με λαλεῖν ἐπέπεσεν τὸ πνεῦμα τὸ ἅγιον ἐπ’ αὐτοὺς ὥσπερ καὶ ἐφ’ ἡμᾶς ἐν ἀρχῇ.

_____

_____

15. Ἐν δὲ τῷ λαλῆσαι ἐρωτᾷ αὐτὸν Φαρισαῖος ὅπως ἀριστήσῃ παρ’ αὐτῷ· εἰσελθὼν δὲ ἀνέπεσεν.

_____

_____

16. Οἶδα γὰρ ὅτι οὐκ οἰκεῖ ἐν ἐμοί, τοῦτ’ ἔστιν ἐν τῇ σαρκί μου, ἀγαθόν· τὸ γὰρ θέλειν παράκειταί μοι, τὸ δὲ κατεργάζεσθαι τὸ καλὸν οὔ.

_____

_____

17. Εὐχαριστεῖν ὀφείλομεν τῷ θεῷ πάντοτε περὶ ὑμῶν, ἀδελφοί, καθὼς ἄξιόν ἐστιν, ὅτι ὑπεραυξάνει ἡ πίστις ὑμῶν καὶ πλεονάζει ἡ ἀγάπη ἑνὸς ἑκάστου πάντων ὑμῶν εἰς ἀλλήλους.

_____

_____

18. οἳ ἀποδώσουσιν λόγον τῷ ἑτοίμως ἔχοντι κρῖναι ζῶντας καὶ νεκρούς.

_____

_____

19. Διαμαρτύρομαι ἐνώπιον τοῦ θεοῦ καὶ Χριστοῦ Ἰησοῦ τοῦ μέλλοντος κρίνειν ζῶντας καὶ νεκρούς, καὶ τὴν ἐπιφάνειαν αὐτοῦ καὶ τὴν βασιλείαν αὐτοῦ.

_____

_____

20. ὑποδείξω δὲ ὑμῖν τίνα φοβηθῆτε· φοβήθητε τὸν μετὰ τὸ ἀποκτεῖναι ἔχοντα ἐξουσίαν ἐμβαλεῖν εἰς τὴν γέενναν. ναὶ λέγω ὑμῖν, τοῦτον φοβήθητε.

_____

_____

22

ADDITIONAL PRONOUNS

GREEK to ENGLISH

Provide the English translation for each Scripture.

1. τινὲς δὲ καὶ τῶν Ἐπικουρείων καὶ Στοϊκῶν φιλοσόφων συνέβαλλον αὐτῷ, καί τινες ἔλεγον· τί ἂν θέλοι ὁ σπερμολόγος οὗτος λέγειν.

   _____

   _____

2. Προσέχετε ἀπὸ τῶν ψευδοπροφητῶν, οἵτινες ἔρχονται πρὸς ὑμᾶς ἐν ἐνδύμασιν προβάτων, ἔσωθεν δέ εἰσιν λύκοι ἅρπαγες.

   _____

   _____

3. ὁ δὲ θέλων δικαιῶσαι ἑαυτὸν εἶπεν πρὸς τὸν Ἰησοῦν· καὶ τίς ἐστίν μου πλησίον;

   _____

   _____

4. πορευθέντες δὲ μάθετε τί ἐστιν· ἔλεος θέλω καὶ οὐ θυσίαν· οὐ γὰρ ἦλθον καλέσαι δικαίους ἀλλὰ ἁμαρτωλούς.

   _____

   _____

5. εἰ δὲ τὸ ζῆν ἐν σαρκί, τοῦτό μοι καρπὸς ἔργου, καὶ τί αἱρήσομαι οὐ γνωρίζω.

   _____

   _____

6. καὶ εὐθὺς ἐπιγνοὺς ὁ Ἰησοῦς τῷ πνεύματι αὐτοῦ ὅτι οὕτως διαλογίζονται ἐν ἑαυτοῖς λέγει αὐτοῖς· τί ταῦτα διαλογίζεσθε ἐν ταῖς καρδίαις ὑμῶν;

   _____

   _____

7. οἱ οὖν ἐν ὑμῖν, φησίν, δυνατοὶ συγκαταβάντες εἴ τί ἐστιν ἐν τῷ ἀνδρὶ ἄτοπον κατηγορείτωσαν αὐτοῦ.

    _____

    _____

8. εἶπεν αὐτοῖς ὁ Ἰησοῦς· εἰ ὁ θεὸς πατὴρ ὑμῶν ἦν ἠγαπᾶτε ἂν ἐμέ, ἐγὼ γὰρ ἐκ τοῦ θεοῦ ἐξῆλθον καὶ ἥκω· οὐδὲ γὰρ ἀπ᾽ ἐμαυτοῦ ἐλήλυθα, ἀλλ᾽ ἐκεῖνός με ἀπέστειλεν.

    _____

    _____

9. σῶσον σεαυτὸν καταβὰς ἀπὸ τοῦ σταυροῦ.

    _____

    _____

10. τί γὰρ οἶδας, γύναι, εἰ τὸν ἄνδρα σώσεις; ἢ τί οἶδας, ἄνερ, εἰ τὴν γυναῖκα σώσεις;

    _____

    _____

11. Πᾶς οὖν ὅστις ἀκούει μου τοὺς λόγους τούτους καὶ ποιεῖ αὐτούς, ὁμοιωθήσεται ἀνδρὶ φρονίμῳ, ὅστις ᾠκοδόμησεν αὐτοῦ τὴν οἰκίαν ἐπὶ τὴν πέτραν.

    _____

    _____

12. εἶπον οὖν αὐτῷ οἱ Φαρισαῖοι· σὺ περὶ σεαυτοῦ μαρτυρεῖς· ἡ μαρτυρία σου οὐκ ἔστιν ἀληθής.

    _____

    _____

13. καὶ εἰ ἐγὼ ἐν Βεελζεβοὺλ ἐκβάλλω τὰ δαιμόνια, οἱ υἱοὶ ὑμῶν ἐν τίνι ἐκβάλλουσιν; διὰ τοῦτο αὐτοὶ κριταὶ ἔσονται ὑμῶν.

    _____

    _____

14. ὅταν γὰρ ἔθνη τὰ μὴ νόμον ἔχοντα φύσει τὰ τοῦ νόμου ποιῶσιν, οὗτοι νόμον μὴ ἔχοντες ἑαυτοῖς εἰσιν νόμος.

_____

_____

15. τοῦ Παύλου ἀπολογουμένου ὅτι οὔτε εἰς τὸν νόμον τῶν Ἰουδαίων οὔτε εἰς τὸ ἱερὸν οὔτε εἰς Καίσαρά τι ἥμαρτον.

_____

_____

16. Ὁμοία γάρ ἐστιν ἡ βασιλεία τῶν οὐρανῶν ἀνθρώπῳ οἰκοδεσπότῃ, ὅστις ἐξῆλθεν ἅμα πρωῒ μισθώσασθαι ἐργάτας εἰς τὸν ἀμπελῶνα αὐτοῦ.

_____

_____

17. πῶς δύνασθε ὑμεῖς πιστεῦσαι δόξαν παρὰ ἀλλήλων λαμβάνοντες, καὶ τὴν δόξαν τὴν παρὰ τοῦ μόνου θεοῦ οὐ ζητεῖτε;

_____

_____

18. ἐγὼ δὲ ἀπεκρίθην· τίς εἶ, κύριε; εἶπέν τε πρός με· ἐγώ εἰμι Ἰησοῦς ὁ Ναζωραῖος, ὃν σὺ διώκεις.

_____

_____

19. οὐ γὰρ τολμήσω τι λαλεῖν ὧν οὐ κατειργάσατο Χριστὸς δι' ἐμοῦ εἰς ὑπακοὴν ἐθνῶν, λόγῳ καὶ ἔργῳ.

_____

_____

20. λέγει αὐτῷ ὁ Ἰησοῦς· πορεύου, ὁ υἱός σου ζῇ. ἐπίστευσεν ὁ ἄνθρωπος τῷ λόγῳ ὃν εἶπεν αὐτῷ ὁ Ἰησοῦς καὶ ἐπορεύετο.

_____

_____

21. καὶ τότε σκανδαλισθήσονται πολλοὶ καὶ ἀλλήλους παραδώσουσιν καὶ μισήσουσιν ἀλλήλους.

_____

_____

22. εἶπεν δὲ ὁ Πέτρος· ἄνθρωπε, οὐκ οἶδα ὃ λέγεις. καὶ παραχρῆμα ἔτι λαλοῦντος αὐτοῦ ἐφώνησεν ἀλέκτωρ.

_____

_____

23. Ἐκ δὲ τῆς πόλεως ἐκείνης πολλοὶ ἐπίστευσαν εἰς αὐτὸν τῶν Σαμαριτῶν διὰ τὸν λόγον τῆς γυναικὸς μαρτυρούσης ὅτι εἶπέν μοι πάντα ἃ ἐποίησα.

_____

_____

24. Ἦσαν δὲ ἐκεῖ γυναῖκες πολλαὶ ἀπὸ μακρόθεν θεωροῦσαι, αἵτινες ἠκολούθησαν τῷ Ἰησοῦ ἀπὸ τῆς Γαλιλαίας διακονοῦσαι αὐτῷ.

_____

_____

25. καὶ μὴ εὑροῦσαι τὸ σῶμα αὐτοῦ ἦλθον λέγουσαι καὶ ὀπτασίαν ἀγγέλων ἑωρακέναι, οἳ λέγουσιν αὐτὸν ζῆν.

_____

_____

26. πέντε γὰρ ἄνδρας ἔσχες καὶ νῦν ὃν ἔχεις οὐκ ἔστιν σου ἀνήρ· τοῦτο ἀληθὲς εἴρηκας.

_____

_____

27. λέγει αὐτῷ ὁ Πιλᾶτος· τί ἐστιν ἀλήθεια; καὶ τοῦτο εἰπὼν πάλιν ἐξῆλθεν πρὸς τοὺς Ἰουδαίους καὶ λέγει αὐτοῖς· ἐγὼ οὐδεμίαν εὑρίσκω ἐν αὐτῷ αἰτίαν.

_____

_____

28. Ἀγαπητοί, εἰ οὕτως ὁ θεὸς ἠγάπησεν ἡμᾶς, καὶ ἡμεῖς ὀφείλομεν ἀλλήλους ἀγαπᾶν.

_____

_____

29. εἴ τις δοκεῖ ἐγνωκέναι τι, οὔπω ἔγνω καθὼς δεῖ γνῶναι.

_____

_____

30. Ἀνέβη δὲ καὶ Ἰωσὴφ ἀπὸ τῆς Γαλιλαίας ἐκ πόλεως Ναζαρὲθ εἰς τὴν Ἰουδαίαν εἰς πόλιν Δαυὶδ ἥτις καλεῖται Βηθλέεμ, διὰ τὸ εἶναι αὐτὸν ἐξ οἴκου καὶ πατριᾶς Δαυίδ.

_____

_____

23

THE SUBJUNCTIVE MOOD

GREEK to ENGLISH

Provide the English translation for each Scripture.

1. Καὶ ἔρχεται πρὸς αὐτὸν λεπρὸς παρακαλῶν αὐτὸν [καὶ γονυπετῶν] καὶ λέγων αὐτῷ ὅτι ἐὰν θέλῃς δύνασαί με καθαρίσαι.

   _____

   _____

2. Ἀδελφοί μου, ἐάν τις ἐν ὑμῖν πλανηθῇ ἀπὸ τῆς ἀληθείας καὶ ἐπιστρέψῃ τις αὐτόν.

   _____

   _____

3. καὶ ἐὰν ἀσπάσησθε τοὺς ἀδελφοὺς ὑμῶν μόνον, τί περισσὸν ποιεῖτε; οὐχὶ καὶ οἱ ἐθνικοὶ τὸ αὐτὸ ποιοῦσιν;

   _____

   _____

4. ὅταν γὰρ ἔθνη τὰ μὴ νόμον ἔχοντα φύσει τὰ τοῦ νόμου ποιῶσιν, οὗτοι νόμον μὴ ἔχοντες ἑαυτοῖς εἰσιν νόμος.

   _____

   _____

5. τοῦ θεοῦ περὶ ἡμῶν κρεῖττόν τι προβλεψαμένου, ἵνα μὴ χωρὶς ἡμῶν τελειωθῶσιν.

   _____

   _____

6. Ὁ λύχνος τοῦ σώματός ἐστιν ὁ ὀφθαλμός. ἐὰν οὖν ᾖ ὁ ὀφθαλμός σου ἁπλοῦς, ὅλον τὸ σῶμά σου φωτεινὸν ἔσται.

   _____

   _____

7. ὅταν ὁ Χριστὸς φανερωθῇ, ἡ ζωὴ ὑμῶν, τότε καὶ ὑμεῖς σὺν αὐτῷ φανερωθήσεσθε ἐν δόξῃ.

_____

_____

8. καὶ ἀποκριθεὶς ὁ Πέτρος λέγει τῷ Ἰησοῦ· ῥαββί, καλόν ἐστιν ἡμᾶς ὧδε εἶναι, καὶ ποιήσωμεν τρεῖς σκηνάς, σοὶ μίαν καὶ Μωϋσεῖ μίαν καὶ Ἠλίᾳ μίαν.

_____

_____

9. καὶ ὃς ἂν μὴ δέξηται ὑμᾶς μηδὲ ἀκούσῃ τοὺς λόγους ὑμῶν, ἐξερχόμενοι ἔξω τῆς οἰκίας ἢ τῆς πόλεως ἐκείνης ἐκτινάξατε τὸν κονιορτὸν τῶν ποδῶν ὑμῶν.

_____

_____

10. κωλυόντων ἡμᾶς τοῖς ἔθνεσιν λαλῆσαι ἵνα σωθῶσιν, εἰς τὸ ἀναπληρῶσαι αὐτῶν τὰς ἁμαρτίας πάντοτε. ἔφθασεν δὲ ἐπ᾽ αὐτοὺς ἡ ὀργὴ εἰς τέλος.

_____

_____

11. Ἐὰν ταῖς γλώσσαις τῶν ἀνθρώπων λαλῶ καὶ τῶν ἀγγέλων, ἀγάπην δὲ μὴ ἔχω, γέγονα χαλκὸς ἠχῶν ἢ κύμβαλον ἀλαλάζον.

_____

_____

12. ὁ δὲ παραδιδοὺς αὐτὸν ἔδωκεν αὐτοῖς σημεῖον λέγων· ὃν ἂν φιλήσω αὐτός ἐστιν, κρατήσατε αὐτόν.

_____

_____

13. ἡμῶν ἐξῆλθαν ἀλλ᾽ οὐκ ἦσαν ἐξ ἡμῶν· εἰ γὰρ ἐξ ἡμῶν ἦσαν, μεμενήκεισαν ἂν μεθ᾽ ἡμῶν· ἀλλ᾽ ἵνα φανερωθῶσιν ὅτι οὐκ εἰσὶν πάντες ἐξ ἡμῶν.

_____

_____

14. ποιήσατε οὖν καρποὺς ἀξίους τῆς μετανοίας καὶ μὴ ἄρξησθε λέγειν ἐν ἑαυτοῖς· πατέρα ἔχομεν τὸν Ἀβραάμ. λέγω γὰρ ὑμῖν ὅτι δύναται ὁ θεὸς ἐκ τῶν λίθων τούτων ἐγεῖραι τέκνα τῷ Ἀβραάμ.

_____

_____

15. ἐὰν γὰρ ἀγαπήσητε τοὺς ἀγαπῶντας ὑμᾶς, τίνα μισθὸν ἔχετε; οὐχὶ καὶ οἱ τελῶναι τὸ αὐτὸ ποιοῦσιν;

_____

_____

16. ὅταν οὖν ἔλθῃ ὁ κύριος τοῦ ἀμπελῶνος, τί ποιήσει τοῖς γεωργοῖς ἐκείνοις;

_____

_____

17. ὥστε ὁ νόμος παιδαγωγὸς ἡμῶν γέγονεν εἰς Χριστόν, ἵνα ἐκ πίστεως δικαιωθῶμεν.

_____

_____

18. καὶ εἰς ἣν ἂν πόλιν εἰσέρχησθε καὶ δέχωνται ὑμᾶς, ἐσθίετε τὰ παρατιθέμενα ὑμῖν.

_____

_____

19. ἐὰν γὰρ εὐαγγελίζωμαι, οὐκ ἔστιν μοι καύχημα· ἀνάγκη γάρ μοι ἐπίκειται· οὐαὶ γάρ μοί ἐστιν ἐὰν μὴ εὐαγγελίσωμαι.

_____

20. Καὶ εἶπεν ὁ Ἰησοῦς· εἰς κρίμα ἐγὼ εἰς τὸν κόσμον τοῦτον ἦλθον, ἵνα οἱ μὴ βλέποντες βλέπωσιν καὶ οἱ βλέποντες τυφλοὶ γένωνται.

_____

_____

21. εἶπεν δὲ αὐτοῖς· ὅταν προσεύχησθε λέγετε· Πάτερ, ἁγιασθήτω τὸ ὄνομά σου· ἐλθέτω ἡ βασιλεία σου.

    _____

    _____

22. Ἔστιν δὲ καὶ ἄλλα πολλὰ ἃ ἐποίησεν ὁ Ἰησοῦς, ἅτινα ἐὰν γράφηται καθ’ ἕν, οὐδ’ αὐτὸν οἶμαι τὸν κόσμον χωρῆσαι τὰ γραφόμενα βιβλία.

    _____

    _____

23. ὑμεῖς δὲ λέγετε· ὃς ἂν εἴπῃ τῷ πατρὶ ἢ τῇ μητρί· δῶρον ὃ ἐὰν ἐξ ἐμοῦ ὠφεληθῇς.

    _____

    _____

24. Βλέπετε οὖν πῶς ἀκούετε· ὃς ἂν γὰρ ἔχῃ, δοθήσεται αὐτῷ· καὶ ὃς ἂν μὴ ἔχῃ, καὶ ὃ δοκεῖ ἔχειν ἀρθήσεται ἀπ’ αὐτοῦ.

    _____

    _____

25. εἶπον οὖν πρὸς αὐτόν· τί ποιῶμεν ἵνα ἐργαζώμεθα τὰ ἔργα τοῦ θεοῦ;

    _____

    _____

26. καὶ ἔσται πᾶς ὃς ἂν ἐπικαλέσηται τὸ ὄνομα κυρίου σωθήσεται.

    _____

    _____

27. μὴ οὖν μεριμνήσητε εἰς τὴν αὔριον, ἡ γὰρ αὔριον μεριμνήσει ἑαυτῆς· ἀρκετὸν τῇ ἡμέρᾳ ἡ κακία αὐτῆς.

    _____

    _____

28. Τὸ οὖν ἀγαθὸν ἐμοὶ ἐγένετο θάνατος; μὴ γένοιτο· ἀλλὰ ἡ ἁμαρτία, ἵνα φανῇ ἁμαρτία, διὰ τοῦ ἀγαθοῦ μοι κατεργαζομένη θάνατον, ἵνα γένηται καθ' ὑπερβολὴν ἁμαρτωλὸς ἡ ἁμαρτία διὰ τῆς ἐντολῆς.

_____

_____

29. ἀμὴν λέγω ὑμῖν ὅτι ὃς ἂν εἴπῃ τῷ ὄρει τούτῳ· ἄρθητι καὶ βλήθητι εἰς τὴν θάλασσαν, καὶ μὴ διακριθῇ ἐν τῇ καρδίᾳ αὐτοῦ ἀλλὰ πιστεύῃ ὅτι ὃ λαλεῖ γίνεται, ἔσται αὐτῷ.

_____

_____

30. καὶ πᾶσα γλῶσσα ἐξομολογήσηται ὅτι κύριος Ἰησοῦς Χριστὸς εἰς δόξαν θεοῦ πατρός.

_____

_____

THE IMPERATIVE AND OPTATIVE MOODS

GREEK to ENGLISH

Provide the English translation for each Scripture.

1. καὶ μὴ φοβεῖσθε ἀπὸ τῶν ἀποκτεννόντων τὸ σῶμα, τὴν δὲ ψυχὴν μὴ δυναμένων ἀποκτεῖναι· φοβεῖσθε δὲ μᾶλλον τὸν δυνάμενον καὶ ψυχὴν καὶ σῶμα ἀπολέσαι ἐν γεέννῃ.

   _____

   _____

2. Ὁ δὲ θεὸς τῆς ἐλπίδος πληρώσαι ὑμᾶς πάσης χαρᾶς καὶ εἰρήνης ἐν τῷ πιστεύειν, εἰς τὸ περισσεύειν ὑμᾶς ἐν τῇ ἐλπίδι ἐν δυνάμει πνεύματος ἁγίου.

   _____

   _____

3. καὶ παρεκάλεσαν αὐτὸν λέγοντες· πέμψον ἡμᾶς εἰς τοὺς χοίρους, ἵνα εἰς αὐτοὺς εἰσέλθωμεν.

   _____

   _____

4. Γίνεσθε δὲ ποιηταὶ λόγου καὶ μὴ μόνον ἀκροαταὶ παραλογιζόμενοι ἑαυτούς.

   _____

   _____

5. εἶπεν οὖν αὐτοῖς ὁ Ἰησοῦς· ἔτι μικρὸν χρόνον τὸ φῶς ἐν ὑμῖν ἐστιν. περιπατεῖτε ὡς τὸ φῶς ἔχετε, ἵνα μὴ σκοτία ὑμᾶς καταλάβῃ· καὶ ὁ περιπατῶν ἐν τῇ σκοτίᾳ οὐκ οἶδεν ποῦ ὑπάγει.

   _____

   _____

6. ἐλθέτω ἡ βασιλεία σου· γενηθήτω τὸ θέλημά σου, ὡς ἐν οὐρανῷ καὶ ἐπὶ γῆς.

    _____

    _____

7. κρεῖττον γὰρ ἀγαθοποιοῦντας, εἰ θέλοι τὸ θέλημα τοῦ θεοῦ, πάσχειν ἢ κακοποιοῦντας.

    _____

    _____

8. αὐτοὶ δὲ ἐπλήσθησαν ἀνοίας καὶ διελάλουν πρὸς ἀλλήλους τί ἂν ποιήσαιεν τῷ Ἰησοῦ.

    _____

    _____

9. μὴ νικῶ ὑπὸ τοῦ κακοῦ ἀλλὰ νίκα ἐν τῷ ἀγαθῷ τὸ κακόν.

    _____

    _____

10. καὶ ἀποκριθεὶς εἶπεν αὐτῇ· μηκέτι εἰς τὸν αἰῶνα ἐκ σοῦ μηδεὶς καρπὸν φάγοι. καὶ ἤκουον οἱ μαθηταὶ αὐτοῦ.

    _____

    _____

11. Προσεύχεσθε περὶ ἡμῶν· πειθόμεθα γὰρ ὅτι καλὴν συνείδησιν ἔχομεν, ἐν πᾶσιν καλῶς θέλοντες ἀναστρέφεσθαι.

    _____

    _____

12. ἐὰν ἐμοί τις διακονῇ, ἐμοὶ ἀκολουθείτω, καὶ ὅπου εἰμὶ ἐγὼ ἐκεῖ καὶ ὁ διάκονος ὁ ἐμὸς ἔσται· ἐάν τις ἐμοὶ διακονῇ τιμήσει αὐτὸν ὁ πατήρ.

    _____

    _____

13. καὶ γὰρ ἐγὼ ἄνθρωπός εἰμι ὑπὸ ἐξουσίαν, ἔχων ὑπ' ἐμαυτὸν στρατιώτας, καὶ λέγω τούτῳ· πορεύθητι, καὶ πορεύεται, καὶ ἄλλῳ· ἔρχου, καὶ ἔρχεται, καὶ τῷ δούλῳ μου· ποίησον τοῦτο, καὶ ποιεῖ.

---

14. ποιήσατε οὖν καρποὺς ἀξίους τῆς μετανοίας καὶ μὴ ἄρξησθε λέγειν ἐν ἑαυτοῖς· πατέρα ἔχομεν τὸν Ἀβραάμ. λέγω γὰρ ὑμῖν ὅτι δύναται ὁ θεὸς ἐκ τῶν λίθων τούτων ἐγεῖραι τέκνα τῷ Ἀβραάμ.

---

15. ἐγείρεσθε ἄγωμεν· ἰδοὺ ὁ παραδιδούς με ἤγγικεν.

---

16. παρακαλέσαι ὑμῶν τὰς καρδίας καὶ στηρίξαι ἐν παντὶ ἔργῳ καὶ λόγῳ ἀγαθῷ.

---

17. οὗτος γάρ ἐστιν ὁ ῥηθεὶς διὰ Ἡσαΐου τοῦ προφήτου λέγοντος· φωνὴ βοῶντος ἐν τῇ ἐρήμῳ· ἑτοιμάσατε τὴν ὁδὸν κυρίου, εὐθείας ποιεῖτε τὰς τρίβους αὐτοῦ.

---

18. τὸ ἐπιεικὲς ὑμῶν γνωσθήτω πᾶσιν ἀνθρώποις. ὁ κύριος ἐγγύς.

---

19. ἐὰν μείνητε ἐν ἐμοὶ καὶ τὰ ῥήματά μου ἐν ὑμῖν μείνῃ, ὃ ἐὰν θέλητε αἰτήσασθε, καὶ γενήσεται ὑμῖν.

---

20. τὰς ἐντολὰς οἶδας· μὴ μοιχεύσῃς, μὴ φονεύσῃς, μὴ κλέψῃς, μὴ ψευδομαρτυρήσῃς, τίμα τὸν πατέρα σου καὶ τὴν μητέρα.

_____

_____

21. καὶ νῦν τί μέλλεις; ἀναστὰς βάπτισαι καὶ ἀπόλουσαι τὰς ἁμαρτίας σου ἐπικαλεσάμενος τὸ ὄνομα αὐτοῦ.

_____

_____

22. ὃ ἐὰν ποιῆτε, ἐκ ψυχῆς ἐργάζεσθε ὡς τῷ κυρίῳ καὶ οὐκ ἀνθρώποις.

_____

_____

23. εἰ οὐ ποιῶ τὰ ἔργα τοῦ πατρός μου, μὴ πιστεύετέ μοι.

_____

_____

24. καὶ λέγει αὐτῷ· εἰ υἱὸς εἶ τοῦ θεοῦ, βάλε σεαυτὸν κάτω· γέγραπται γὰρ ὅτι τοῖς ἀγγέλοις αὐτοῦ ἐντελεῖται περὶ σοῦ καὶ ἐπὶ χειρῶν ἀροῦσίν σε, μήποτε προσκόψῃς πρὸς λίθον τὸν πόδα (foot) σου.

_____

_____

25. ἀκούσας δὲ ὄχλου διαπορευομένου ἐπυνθάνετο τί εἴη τοῦτο.

_____

_____

26. Ἀσπάσασθε Πρίσκαν καὶ Ἀκύλαν τοὺς συνεργούς μου ἐν Χριστῷ Ἰησοῦ.

_____

_____

27. πᾶς λόγος σαπρὸς ἐκ τοῦ στόματος ὑμῶν μὴ ἐκπορευέσθω, ἀλλὰ εἴ τις ἀγαθὸς πρὸς οἰκοδομὴν τῆς χρείας, ἵνα δῷ χάριν τοῖς ἀκούουσιν.

_____

_____

28. καὶ προσῆλθεν ὁ Ἰησοῦς καὶ ἁψάμενος αὐτῶν εἶπεν· ἐγέρθητε καὶ μὴ φοβεῖσθε.

_____

_____

29. ἀλλ' εἰ καὶ πάσχοιτε διὰ δικαιοσύνην, μακάριοι. τὸν δὲ φόβον αὐτῶν μὴ φοβηθῆτε μηδὲ ταραχθῆτε.

_____

_____

30. ἀποκριθεὶς δὲ ὁ ἀρχισυνάγωγος, ἀγανακτῶν ὅτι τῷ σαββάτῳ ἐθεράπευσεν ὁ Ἰησοῦς, ἔλεγεν τῷ ὄχλῳ ὅτι ἓξ ἡμέραι εἰσὶν ἐν αἷς δεῖ ἐργάζεσθαι· ἐν αὐταῖς οὖν ἐρχόμενοι θεραπεύεσθε καὶ μὴ τῇ ἡμέρᾳ τοῦ σαββάτου.

_____

_____

THE CONJUGATION OF -μι VERBS

GREEK to ENGLISH

Provide the English translation for each Scripture.

1. χάρις δὲ τῷ θεῷ ὅτι ἦτε δοῦλοι τῆς ἁμαρτίας ὑπηκούσατε δὲ ἐκ καρδίας εἰς ὃν παρεδόθητε τύπον διδαχῆς.

———————————————————————————

———————————————————————————

2. σὺ δὲ ὅταν προσεύχῃ, εἴσελθε εἰς τὸ ταμεῖόν σου καὶ κλείσας τὴν θύραν σου πρόσευξαι τῷ πατρί σου τῷ ἐν τῷ κρυπτῷ· καὶ ὁ πατήρ σου ὁ βλέπων ἐν τῷ κρυπτῷ ἀποδώσει σοι.

———————————————————————————

———————————————————————————

3. εἶπεν δὲ πρὸς αὐτούς· τίνες οἱ λόγοι οὗτοι οὓς ἀντιβάλλετε πρὸς ἀλλήλους περιπατοῦντες; καὶ ἐστάθησαν σκυθρωποί.

———————————————————————————

———————————————————————————

4. καθὼς ἔδωκας αὐτῷ ἐξουσίαν πάσης σαρκός, ἵνα πᾶν ὃ δέδωκας αὐτῷ δώσῃ αὐτοῖς ζωὴν αἰώνιον.

———————————————————————————

———————————————————————————

5. ἔφη τε ὁ Παῦλος· οὐκ ᾔδειν, ἀδελφοί, ὅτι ἐστὶν ἀρχιερεύς· γέγραπται γὰρ ὅτι ἄρχοντα τοῦ λαοῦ σου οὐκ ἐρεῖς κακῶς.

———————————————————————————

———————————————————————————

6. Διὰ τοῦτο λέγω ὑμῖν, πᾶσα ἁμαρτία καὶ βλασφημία ἀφεθήσεται τοῖς ἀνθρώποις, ἡ δὲ τοῦ πνεύματος βλασφημία οὐκ ἀφεθήσεται.

_____

_____

7. ἰδοὺ ἀφίεται ὑμῖν ὁ οἶκος ὑμῶν. λέγω (δὲ) ὑμῖν, οὐ μὴ ἴδητέ με ἕως (ἥξει ὅτε) εἴπητε· εὐλογημένος ὁ ἐρχόμενος ἐν ὀνόματι κυρίου.

_____

_____

8. καὶ ἰδὼν ὁ Ἰησοῦς τὴν πίστιν αὐτῶν λέγει τῷ παραλυτικῷ· τέκνον, ἀφίενταί σου αἱ ἁμαρτίαι.

_____

_____

9. καὶ ἔθεντο πάντες οἱ ἀκούσαντες ἐν τῇ καρδίᾳ αὐτῶν λέγοντες· τί ἄρα τὸ παιδίον τοῦτο ἔσται; καὶ γὰρ χεὶρ κυρίου ἦν μετ’ αὐτοῦ.

_____

_____

10. καὶ ἤρχοντο πρὸς αὐτὸν καὶ ἔλεγον· χαῖρε ὁ βασιλεὺς τῶν Ἰουδαίων· καὶ ἐδίδοσαν αὐτῷ ῥαπίσματα.

_____

_____

11. καὶ εὑρὼν ἐπιτίθησιν ἐπὶ τοὺς ὤμους αὐτοῦ.

_____

_____

12. Ἐάν τις ἴδῃ τὸν ἀδελφὸν αὐτοῦ ἁμαρτάνοντα ἁμαρτίαν μὴ πρὸς θάνατον, αἰτήσει καὶ δώσει αὐτῷ ζωήν, τοῖς ἁμαρτάνουσιν μὴ πρὸς θάνατον. ἔστιν ἁμαρτία πρὸς θάνατον· οὐ περὶ ἐκείνης λέγω ἵνα ἐρωτήσῃ.

_____

_____

13. ἰδοὺ ἀναβαίνομεν εἰς Ἱεροσόλυμα, καὶ ὁ υἱὸς τοῦ ἀνθρώπου παραδοθήσεται τοῖς ἀρχιερεῦσιν καὶ γραμματεῦσιν, καὶ κατακρινοῦσιν αὐτὸν θανάτῳ.

_____

_____

14. οὐαὶ αὐτοῖς, ὅτι τῇ ὁδῷ τοῦ Κάϊν ἐπορεύθησαν καὶ τῇ πλάνῃ τοῦ Βαλαὰμ μισθοῦ ἐξεχύθησαν καὶ τῇ ἀντιλογίᾳ τοῦ Κόρε ἀπώλοντο.

_____

_____

15. ἀποκριθεὶς δὲ ὁ Ἰησοῦς εἶπεν πρὸς αὐτόν· ἄφες ἄρτι, οὕτως γὰρ πρέπον ἐστὶν ἡμῖν πληρῶσαι πᾶσαν δικαιοσύνην. τότε ἀφίησιν αὐτόν.

_____

_____

16. ἐλθὼν ἔφη· πόσοι μίσθιοι τοῦ πατρός μου περισσεύονται ἄρτων, ἐγὼ δὲ λιμῷ ὧδε ἀπόλλυμαι.

_____

_____

17. μετὰ τοῦτον ἀνέστη Ἰούδας ὁ Γαλιλαῖος ἐν ταῖς ἡμέραις τῆς ἀπογραφῆς καὶ ἀπέστησεν λαὸν ὀπίσω αὐτοῦ· κἀκεῖνος ἀπώλετο καὶ πάντες ὅσοι ἐπείθοντο αὐτῷ διεσκορπίσθησαν.

_____

_____

18. Ἐγὼ γὰρ παρέλαβον ἀπὸ τοῦ κυρίου, ὃ καὶ παρέδωκα ὑμῖν, ὅτι ὁ κύριος Ἰησοῦς ἐν τῇ νυκτὶ ᾗ παρεδίδετο ἔλαβεν ἄρτον.

_____

_____

19. Ἑνὶ δὲ ἑκάστῳ ἡμῶν ἐδόθη ἡ χάρις κατὰ τὸ μέτρον τῆς δωρεᾶς τοῦ Χριστοῦ.

_____

_____

20. ἵνα δὲ εἰδῆτε ὅτι ὁ υἱὸς τοῦ ἀνθρώπου ἐξουσίαν ἔχει ἐπὶ τῆς γῆς ἀφιέναι ἁμαρτίας εἶπεν τῷ παραλελυμένῳ· σοὶ λέγω, ἔγειρε καὶ ἄρας τὸ κλινίδιόν σου πορεύου εἰς τὸν οἶκόν σου.

_____

_____

21. διότι ἐγώ εἰμι μετὰ σοῦ καὶ οὐδεὶς ἐπιθήσεταί σοι τοῦ κακῶσαί σε, διότι λαός ἐστί μοι πολὺς ἐν τῇ πόλει ταύτῃ.

_____

_____

22. Τότε παραλαμβάνει αὐτὸν ὁ διάβολος εἰς τὴν ἁγίαν πόλιν καὶ ἔστησεν αὐτὸν ἐπὶ τὸ πτερύγιον τοῦ ἱεροῦ.

_____

_____

23. καὶ οὐδεὶς βάλλει οἶνον νέον εἰς ἀσκοὺς παλαιούς· εἰ δὲ μή γε, ῥήξει ὁ οἶνος ὁ νέος τοὺς ἀσκοὺς καὶ αὐτὸς ἐκχυθήσεται καὶ οἱ ἀσκοὶ ἀπολοῦνται.

_____

_____

24. Μωϋσῆς μὲν εἶπεν ὅτι προφήτην ὑμῖν ἀναστήσει κύριος ὁ θεὸς ὑμῶν ἐκ τῶν ἀδελφῶν ὑμῶν ὡς ἐμέ· αὐτοῦ ἀκούσεσθε κατὰ πάντα ὅσα ἂν λαλήσῃ πρὸς ὑμᾶς.

_____

_____

25. Πάλιν παραλαμβάνει αὐτὸν ὁ διάβολος εἰς ὄρος ὑψηλὸν λίαν καὶ δείκνυσιν αὐτῷ πάσας τὰς βασιλείας τοῦ κόσμου καὶ τὴν δόξαν αὐτῶν.

_____

_____

26. Τρίτον τοῦτο ἔρχομαι πρὸς ὑμᾶς· ἐπὶ στόματος δύο μαρτύρων καὶ τριῶν σταθήσεται πᾶν ῥῆμα.

_____

_____

27. ἑπτὰ ἀδελφοὶ ἦσαν· καὶ ὁ πρῶτος ἔλαβεν γυναῖκα καὶ ἀποθνήσκων οὐκ ἀφῆκεν σπέρμα.

_____

_____

28. Εἰ μὲν οὖν τελείωσις διὰ τῆς Λευιτικῆς ἱερωσύνης ἦν, ὁ λαὸς γὰρ ἐπ᾽ αὐτῆς νενομοθέτηται, τίς ἔτι χρεία κατὰ τὴν τάξιν Μελχισέδεκ ἕτερον ἀνίστασθαι ἱερέα καὶ οὐ κατὰ τὴν τάξιν Ἀαρὼν λέγεσθαι;

_____

_____

29. Ὅσοι γὰρ ἀνόμως ἥμαρτον, ἀνόμως καὶ ἀπολοῦνται, καὶ ὅσοι ἐν νόμῳ ἥμαρτον, διὰ νόμου κριθήσονται.

_____

_____

30. μηδὲ ἐκπειράζωμεν τὸν Χριστόν, καθώς τινες αὐτῶν ἐπείρασαν καὶ ὑπὸ τῶν ὄφεων ἀπώλλυντο.

_____

_____

INDICATIVE VERB CHART

λύω	Active	Middle	Passive
Present			
Future			ALSO NO Ø
Imperfect			

λύω	Active	Middle	Passive
Aorist	___ ___ ___ ___ ___ ___ ___ ___ ___ ___ ___ ___ ___ ___	___ ___ ___ ___ ___ ___ ___ ___ ___ ___ ___ ___ ___ ___ ___ ___ ___ ___	___ ___ ___ ___ ___ ___ ___ ___ ___ ___ NO Ø
Perfect	___ ___ ___ ___ ___ ___ ___ ALSO NO Ø	___ ___ ___ ___ ___	___ ___ ___
Pluperfect	___ ___ ___ ___ ___ ___ ___	___ ___ ___ ___ ___ ___	___ ___

Forms of ἐιμί

Present Indicative

_____   _____

_____   _____

_____   _____

Future Indicative

_____   _____

_____   _____

_____   _____

Imperfect Indicative

_____   _____

_____   _____

_____   _____

PARTICIPLE CHART

λύω	Active		Middle		Passive	
Perfect						
1st Aorist						
2nd Aorist						

ALSO

λύω	Active		Middle		Passive	
Perfect						
Future						

Forms of εἰμί

Participle

Appendix C

INFINITIVE, IMPERATIVE, AND SUBJUNCTIVE CHARTS

INFINITIVE VERB CHART

λύω	Active	Middle	Passive
Present	_____	_____	
1st Aorist	_____	_____	_____
2nd Aorist	_____	_____	_____
Perfect	_____	_____	

IMPERATIVE VERB CHART

λύω	Active	Middle	Passive
Present	____ ____ ____ ____	_____ _____	____ ____ ____ ____
1st Aorist	____ ____ ____ ____	____ ____ ____ ____	____ ____ ____ ____
2nd Aorist	____ ____ ____ ____	____ ____ ____ ____	____ ____ ____ ____

SUBJUNCTIVE VERB CHART

λύω	Active	Middle	Passive
Present			
1st Aorist			
2nd Aorist			
1st Perfect			
2nd Perfect			

Forms of εἰμί

Present Infinitive

_____

Future Infinitive

_____

Present Subjunctive

_____   _____

_____   _____

_____   _____

Present Imperative

_____   _____

_____   _____